The Investigator's Guide to Online Resources:

Uncovering Financial Fraud and Crimes in the Digital Age

Ann Adams

@Copyright 2024 Ann Adams - All rights reserved

No part of this book may be reproduced, or stored in a retrieval system, or transmitted in any form or by any means, electronic, mechanical, photocopying, recording, or otherwise, without express written permission of the publisher.

The views expressed in this book are those of the author and do not necessarily reflect the views of the publisher. The mention of specific companies or certain products does not constitute an endorsement by the author or publisher.

The information in this book is provided "as is" and without warranties of any kind, either express or implied. To the fullest extent permissible pursuant to applicable law, the author and publisher disclaim all warranties, express or implied, including, but not limited to, implied warranties of merchantability and fitness for a particular purpose. The author and publisher do not warrant that the contents of this book are error-free.

All trademarks and registered trademarks appearing in this book are the property of their respective owners.

By using this book, the reader agrees to the terms and conditions stated above. If you do not agree with these terms and conditions, please do not use this book.

Cover design by: Ann Adams

The Investigator's Guide to Online Resources: Uncovering Financial Fraud and Crimes in the Digital Age

"The internet is the world's largest library, but all the books are on the floor." - John Allen Paulos

In the intricate world of financial investigations, "The Investigator's Guide to Online Resources " emerges as a critical guidebook, unlocking the digital universe's vast potential in uncovering financial deceptions. Crafted meticulously by Ann Adams, this comprehensive book serves as a beacon for anyone embarking on the challenging journey of online financial scrutiny.

Dive deep into the heart of cyber-financial activities, exploring the evolution of financial investigations in the digital age. From mastering Open Source Intelligence (OSINT) techniques to dissecting the complexities of digital payment systems and cryptocurrency, this guide is an indispensable resource for both novices and seasoned professionals. Navigate through chapters dedicated to unmasking the actors behind financial schemes, leveraging advanced investigative techniques, and ensuring the admissibility of digital evidence.

This book not only equips readers with the technical skills necessary for digital financial investigations but also emphasizes the importance of ethical considerations, guiding investigators to operate within legal frameworks. Whether you're a law enforcement officer, a financial analyst, or an individual keen on understanding the nexus between finance and technology, this book is your comprehensive guide in the vast sea of digital information.

Key Features:

- In-depth exploration of OSINT techniques and their application in financial investigations.

- Comprehensive insights into digital payment systems and cryptocurrencies, including investigative strategies for tracing digital transactions.

- Detailed guidance on building profiles, utilizing advanced investigative techniques, and navigating legal challenges in digital financial investigations.

- Real-world case studies illustrating the application of investigative techniques in various contexts.

Embark on a journey of discovery and mastery with "The Investigator's Guide to Online Resources." Unveil the secrets of the digital world and arm yourself with the knowledge and skills to combat financial crimes effectively in the digital age.

Table of Contents

Introduction 10

Chapter 1: The Evolving Landscape of Financial Investigations 13

    1.1 The Rise of Cybercrime 14

    1.2 The Importance of Digital Evidence 18

    1.3 Tools and Technologies for Digital Investigations 20

    1.4 Building a Digital Investigative Team 22

    1.5 Developing a Digital Investigation Strategy 25

Chapter 2: Mastering Open Source Intelligence (OSINT) Techniques 28

    2.1 Understanding OSINT and its Value 31

    2.2 Utilizing Search Engines and Social Media Platforms 33

    2.3 Exploring Public Records and Databases 44

    2.4 Extracting Information from Websites and Online Forums 46

    2.5 Verifying and Analyzing OSINT Data 48

Chapter 3: Tracing the Money: Digital Payment Systems and Cryptocurrency Investigations 50

    3.1 Understanding Digital Payment Systems 53

    3.2 Demystifying Cryptocurrency 55

    3.3 Investigating Cryptocurrency Exchanges and Wallets 61

    3.4 Utilizing Blockchain Forensics 63

    3.5 Building a Cryptocurrency Investigation Strategy .. 65

Chapter 4: Unmasking the Actors: Identifying and Profiling Individuals and Organizations 71

    4.1 Utilizing Online Data for Identification 73

    4.2 Investigating Corporate Structures and Ownership 77

    4.3 Leveraging Network Analysis and Link Charts 82

    4.4 Understanding Behavioral Patterns and Motivations 84

    4.5 Building Comprehensive Profiles 86

Chapter 5: Diving Deeper: Utilizing Advanced Investigative Techniques 89

    5.1 Utilizing Data Mining and Analytics........................ 91

    5.2 Mastering Digital Forensics 97

    5.3 Conducting Covert Online Investigations 101

    5.4 Leveraging Social Engineering Techniques 103

    5.5 Integrating Advanced Techniques into Investigations 105

Chapter 6: Navigating the Legal Landscape: Data Privacy, Regulations, and International Cooperation. 108

    6.1 Understanding Data Privacy Laws 111

    6.2 Complying with Financial Regulations.................... 113

    6.3 Obtaining Legal Assistance and Cooperation 115

    6.4 Handling Evidence and Ensuring Admissibility 117

    6.5 Balancing Investigative Needs with Privacy Rights 119

Chapter 7: Building a Case: Evidence Collection, Preservation, and Presentation 121

    7.1 Developing an Evidence Collection Plan 123

    7.2 Ensuring Proper Chain of Custody.......................... 128

    7.3 Preserving Digital Evidence..................................... 133

    7.4 Analyzing and Interpreting Evidence 135

    7.5 Presenting Evidence Effectively 136

Chapter 8: The Future of Financial Investigations: Emerging Technologies and Trends 141

    8.1 The Rise of Artificial Intelligence and Machine Learning.. 143

    8.2 Blockchain Technology and its Impact.................... 146

8.3 The Growing Importance of Cybersecurity............148
8.4 The Need for Continuous Learning and Adaptation
....157
8.5 Shaping the Future of Financial Investigations......159

Conclusion..*162*

References..*166*

Introduction

In an age where digital footprints are as revealing as physical ones, "The Investigator's Guide to Online Resources" stands as a crucial guide for anyone venturing into the intricate world of online financial scrutiny. As the internet burgeons into an expansive arena of information and interaction, it simultaneously morphs into a labyrinthine space ripe for financial misdemeanors and complexities. This book offers a compass for navigating this digital terrain, providing readers with the acumen to harness the internet's vast potential in unveiling financial deceptions and ensuring accountability.

In the chapters that follow, you will embark on a comprehensive journey, exploring the evolution of financial investigations in the digital age. From the basic tenets of internet usage to advanced investigative techniques, this guide illuminates the path for both novices and seasoned professionals. It delves into the core of cyber-financial activities, elucidating the mechanisms of online transactions, cryptocurrency nuances, and the digital trails left by financial transactions.

This introduction serves as your portal to understanding the multifaceted role of the internet in financial investigations. It beckons you to peer beyond the surface, to explore not just the 'how' but the 'why' of online financial investigations. As we traverse through the chapters, we unravel the methodologies that empower investigators to track, analyze, and interpret digital data effectively, transforming raw information into actionable insights.

Moreover, this book is not just a technical manual; it's a narrative that intertwines the empirical with the ethical, guiding readers through the legal frameworks and moral compasses necessary in the digital investigation realm. It addresses the burgeoning challenges that cyber-financial activities pose, offering strategies to adapt and thrive in this ever-evolving landscape.

As you turn these pages, you'll gain not just knowledge but a perspective, one that views the internet not as a daunting expanse but as a fertile ground for investigation and enlightenment. Whether you're a law enforcement officer, a financial analyst, or an inquisitive mind keen on understanding the nexus between finance and technology, this book is your beacon in the vast sea of digital information.

Chapter 1: The Evolving Landscape of Financial Investigations

In 2022, global cybercrime damages exceeded $8.44 trillion. - Uknown

Welcome to the digital age – a remarkable era where technology's rapid evolution has redefined our lives, our interactions, and the very fabric of society. Yet, beneath this digital veneer lies a shadowy underbelly, a realm where the anonymity and vastness of the internet serve as a double-edged sword. This is the world of cybercrime – a complex, ever-evolving threat landscape that poses unique challenges and demands a new caliber of vigilance and expertise.

As we delve into this chapter, we embark on a comprehensive journey to uncover the intricacies of financial investigations in the digital realm. This exploration is not just about understanding the nature of cybercrime; it's about equipping ourselves with the knowledge and tools to navigate this intricate digital quagmire.

We live in a time where the line between the physical and digital worlds blurs, where financial transactions, personal data, and corporate secrets traverse the globe in milliseconds. In this interconnected environment, cybercrime has emerged as a formidable adversary, with financial fraud, data breaches, and identity theft becoming all too common.

Yet, with challenge comes opportunity. This chapter aims to illuminate the path for financial investigators, law enforcement professionals, and anyone keen on understanding or combating digital financial crime. We'll explore the technological advancements and investigative techniques that are turning the tide against cybercriminals, offering a beacon of hope in the fight to secure our digital frontiers.

So, let's embark on this enlightening journey together, unraveling the complexities of cybercrime, understanding the tools at our disposal, and forging a path toward a more secure digital future. The realm of financial investigations is vast and intricate, but with the right knowledge and skills, we can navigate it with confidence and acumen.

1.1 The Rise of Cybercrime

As the internet has become an integral part of our lives, it has also become a fertile ground for criminal activity. Cybercrime has exploded in recent years, with financial crimes constituting a significant portion of this illicit activity. The anonymity and borderless nature of the internet present unique challenges for investigators seeking to trace financial crimes and bring perpetrators to justice.

In an era where digital footprints are the norm and the internet weaves through the fabric of our daily lives, cybercrime has burgeoned, morphing into a pervasive threat that challenges individuals, corporations, and nations alike. The ascent of cybercrime is not just a statistic; it's a vivid narrative of evolving threats and the constant battle between security and exploitation.

The year 2022 bore witness to an unprecedented escalation in cybercrime, with global damages exceeding a staggering $8.44 trillion, painting a grim tableau of the digital age's dark underbelly. The anonymity and borderless expanse of the internet have furnished malefactors with a potent arsenal to orchestrate crimes from remote sanctuaries, evading traditional mechanisms of law enforcement and jurisdictional boundaries.

Cybercrime's canvas is vast, spanning from intricate phishing expeditions to elaborate ransomware sieges. The internet's dual-edged sword facilitates not only groundbreaking innovations but also a playground for fraudsters exploiting every conceivable digital loophole. These nefarious activities include:

1. **Fraud**: Cyber fraud manifests in myriad forms, from sophisticated phishing scams ensnaring unsuspecting victims to elaborate identity theft schemes. In 2023 alone, a sophisticated phishing campaign orchestrated by a cyber syndicate mimicked a reputable bank's communication, duping customers into divulging critical financial data.

2. **Money Laundering**: The digital realm has revolutionized traditional money laundering methodologies. Cybercriminals now launder illicit funds through complex webs of online transactions, utilizing cryptocurrencies and digital platforms to obscure the origins of their ill-gotten gains.

3. **Data Breaches**: The theft of sensitive data is a cornerstone of cybercrime, with attackers targeting corporate databases to pilfer personal information, trade secrets, and financial data, subsequently traded in the dark recesses of the internet.

4. **Ransomware**: This insidious form of cyber extortion involves infiltrating and encrypting an organization's digital assets, demanding hefty ransoms for data restoration. The proliferation of cryptocurrencies has further emboldened such attacks, enabling anonymous transactions between attackers and victims.

5. **Dark Web Marketplaces**: The dark web serves as a clandestine marketplace for trading stolen data, illegal software, and various contraband. This shadowy digital bazaar is a testament to the internet's dark side, accessible only via specialized tools designed to preserve anonymity.

The transnational nature of cybercrime poses unique challenges, transcending traditional borders and jurisdictional confines. International collaboration and real-time intelligence sharing become imperative in this relentless battle against digital crime syndicates.

To fortify against this relentless tide of cybercrime, individuals and organizations must adopt a proactive stance. Vigilance, advanced cybersecurity measures, and continuous education about emerging cyber threats are crucial bulwarks against this digital onslaught.

As we navigate this tumultuous digital landscape, understanding the multifaceted nature of cybercrime is paramount. Our collective resilience, innovative countermeasures, and unwavering commitment to cybersecurity can illuminate the path forward, transforming this challenging scenario into a narrative of triumph over adversity.

By delving into the intricacies of cybercrime, we not only enhance our defenses but also forge a future where digital spaces are bastions of security and trust. The journey is complex, but with informed strategies and collaborative efforts, we can turn the tide against the specter of cybercrime, safeguarding our digital horizons for generations to come.

1.2 The Importance of Digital Evidence

In the digital age, financial crimes often leave behind a trail of digital evidence. This evidence can be crucial in reconstructing events, identifying perpetrators, and building a solid case. Digital footprints can reveal a wealth of information about financial transactions, communications, and online activities.

Digital evidence can take many forms, including:

Transaction logs: Records of financial transactions, including dates, amounts, and parties involved.

Emails and messages: Communications between suspects and victims, often containing incriminating information.

Internet browsing history: Websites visited and searches conducted, providing insights into the suspect's activities and interests.

Social media posts and interactions: Online activity that can reveal connections, locations, and potential motives.

Digital files and documents: Financial records, spreadsheets, and other documents that can provide evidence of wrongdoing.

The ability to find, collect, and analyze digital evidence is essential for financial investigators. This requires a combination of technical skills, legal knowledge, and investigative expertise. Investigators must be familiar with various digital forensic tools and techniques to extract and analyze data from computers, mobile devices, and online platforms.

However, collecting and using digital evidence also raises legal and ethical considerations. Investigators must ensure that they obtain proper authorization and follow established procedures to maintain the integrity and admissibility of evidence. Failure to do so can jeopardize the entire case.

Consider a case where investigators are looking into suspected embezzlement from a company. By analyzing the suspect's computer and financial records, they discover deleted emails discussing the transfer of funds to a personal account. This digital evidence becomes crucial in proving the suspect's guilt and recovering the stolen funds.

Have you ever considered the digital trail you leave behind in your daily online activities? How can this information be used in an investigation?

Take steps to be mindful of your digital footprint and protect your privacy online. If you are involved in a financial investigation, it is crucial to seek legal counsel and cooperate with investigators to ensure that your rights are protected and that evidence is handled properly.

Digital evidence plays a critical role in modern financial investigations. Investigators who are adept at finding, collecting, and analyzing digital evidence will be better equipped to uncover financial crimes, identify perpetrators, and build strong cases. However, it is essential to ensure that digital evidence is collected and handled in a way that preserves its integrity and admissibility in court.

1.3 Tools and Technologies for Digital Investigations

The increasing complexity of financial crimes and the growing importance of digital evidence have led to the development of a wide range of tools and technologies specifically designed for digital investigations. These tools assist investigators in finding, collecting, analyzing, and presenting digital evidence effectively.

Some of the commonly used tools and technologies in digital financial investigations include:

Data mining and analytics software: These tools allow investigators to analyze large datasets, identify patterns, and detect anomalies that may indicate fraudulent activity.

Digital forensic tools: These tools enable investigators to recover deleted data, crack passwords, and analyze digital files and devices to extract evidence.

Network analysis and visualization tools: These tools help investigators visualize relationships between individuals, organizations, and financial transactions, revealing hidden connections and networks.

Blockchain forensic tools: These tools are specifically designed to trace cryptocurrency transactions and analyze blockchain data to identify suspicious activities.

Social media monitoring tools: These tools allow investigators to track online activity, identify potential leads, and gather evidence from social media platforms.

While these tools and technologies offer significant advantages for investigators, it is important to note that they also raise ethical and legal considerations. Some tools may be intrusive and require proper authorization to use. Investigators must be aware of the legal and ethical implications of using these tools and ensure that they comply with all applicable laws and regulations.

For example, investigators might use data mining software to analyze a large dataset of financial transactions. The software can identify unusual patterns or transactions that deviate from the norm, potentially indicating fraudulent activity. This can help investigators focus their investigation and identify potential leads.

Have you ever used any data analysis or digital forensic tools? How can these tools be used responsibly and ethically in investigations?

It is important to stay informed about the latest tools and technologies available for digital investigations and to receive proper training in their use. Investigators should also be aware of the legal and ethical considerations associated with these tools and ensure that they are used responsibly and in compliance with the law.

The use of appropriate tools and technologies can significantly enhance the effectiveness of digital financial investigations. By leveraging these tools, investigators can uncover hidden evidence, identify perpetrators, and build stronger cases. However, it is crucial to use these tools responsibly and ethically, ensuring compliance with all legal and regulatory requirements.

1.4 Building a Digital Investigative Team

Conducting effective digital financial investigations often requires a diverse team of experts with complementary skills and knowledge. Building a strong team is crucial for navigating the complexities of digital evidence, financial transactions, and legal considerations.

A well-rounded digital investigative team typically includes:

Financial experts: Individuals with expertise in accounting, financial analysis, and fraud detection. They can analyze financial records, identify irregularities, and trace the flow of funds.

Cybersecurity professionals: Experts in digital forensics, network analysis, and cybersecurity tools. They can collect and analyze digital evidence, identify cybercrime tactics, and secure data.

Legal professionals: Lawyers and legal advisors who can provide guidance on legal matters, ensure compliance with regulations, and assist with obtaining warrants and other legal instruments.

Investigators: Individuals with experience in conducting investigations, interviewing witnesses, and gathering evidence. They can lead the investigation, interview suspects, and build a case.

In some cases, it may be necessary to involve additional specialists, such as cryptocurrency experts, data scientists, or social engineering specialists. The size and composition of the team will depend on the specific nature and complexity of the investigation.

Collaboration and communication are essential for a digital investigative team to function effectively. Team members must share information, coordinate their efforts, and work together to achieve the investigation's objectives.

For example, in a case involving cryptocurrency fraud, a financial expert might analyze blockchain data to trace the flow of funds, while a cybersecurity professional might conduct digital forensics on the suspect's computer to identify evidence of the crime. A legal professional would ensure that all evidence is collected and handled in a way that complies with the law, and an investigator would lead the overall investigation and interview witnesses.

What skills and expertise do you think are most important for a digital investigator to possess?

Building a strong and diverse team with complementary skills and expertise is crucial for conducting effective digital financial investigations. Collaboration, communication, and a shared commitment to uncovering the truth are essential for success.

By bringing together individuals with diverse backgrounds and expertise, investigative teams can effectively navigate the complexities of digital financial crimes and build strong cases that bring perpetrators to justice.

1.5 Developing a Digital Investigation Strategy

A well-defined and comprehensive investigation strategy is crucial for the success of any digital financial investigation. The strategy should be tailored to the specific case and objectives, taking into account the nature of the crime, the available resources, and the legal and regulatory environment.

Key steps involved in developing a digital investigation strategy include:

Case assessment: Define the scope of the investigation, identify the key questions that need to be answered, and determine the desired outcome.

Risk assessment: Identify potential risks and challenges associated with the investigation, such as data privacy concerns, legal hurdles, and the potential for data loss or destruction.

Resource allocation: Determine the necessary resources, including personnel, technology, and funding, and allocate them effectively.

Methodology selection: Choose the appropriate investigative methods and tools based on the nature of the crime and the available evidence.

Timeline development: Establish a timeline of events and prioritize investigative tasks.

Chain of custody procedures: Implement strict chain of custody procedures to ensure the integrity and admissibility of evidence.

Communication plan: Establish clear communication channels and protocols for sharing information within the investigative team and with external stakeholders.

Contingency planning: Anticipate potential roadblocks and develop contingency plans to address them.

Throughout the investigation, the strategy should be reviewed and updated regularly to reflect new information and developments. Flexibility and adaptability are crucial in digital investigations, as new evidence and challenges can emerge unexpectedly.

For example, in a case involving online fraud, the investigation strategy might involve analyzing financial transactions, tracing IP addresses, and conducting undercover online operations. The strategy would also need to address legal considerations, such as obtaining warrants and ensuring the admissibility of evidence.

What are some of the key considerations you would take into account when developing a digital investigation strategy?

Developing a comprehensive and adaptable investigation strategy is essential for navigating the complexities of digital financial investigations. By carefully considering the case objectives, potential risks, available resources, and legal requirements, investigators can increase their chances of success and bring perpetrators to justice.

Chapter 2: Mastering Open Source Intelligence (OSINT) Techniques

"The best place to hide a secret is in plain sight." - Edgar Allan Poe

In the labyrinthine world of financial investigations, the advent of Open Source Intelligence (OSINT) has emerged as a lighthouse, guiding investigators through the murky waters of digital data. This chapter is an odyssey into the realm of OSINT, a domain where publicly accessible information becomes the cornerstone of unraveling complex financial crimes.

The digital age has ushered in an era of unprecedented data proliferation. Every digital footprint, every online interaction, and every electronic transaction creates a repository of information. While this abundance of data may seem overwhelming, it holds the keys to unlocking patterns, relationships, and activities that are pivotal in financial investigations. Herein lies the essence of OSINT – the art and science of transforming publicly available data into actionable intelligence.

Financial crimes have evolved, becoming more sophisticated and intricate. The perpetrators operate in the shadows of the digital world, leveraging the anonymity and vastness of the internet to conduct their illicit activities. In this complex landscape, traditional investigative methods alone are no longer sufficient. OSINT provides the tools and methodologies to augment these traditional approaches, offering a panoramic view of the digital traces left by financial criminals.

OSINT is not merely about collecting data; it's about discerning the signal in the noise. It involves sifting through vast quantities of information to identify relevant data points that can be pieced together to form a coherent narrative. In the context of financial investigations, this could mean tracing the origins of suspicious transactions, uncovering hidden connections between entities, or revealing the financial networks that fuel illicit activities.

At its core, OSINT encompasses a myriad of dimensions. It involves scouring the internet, social media platforms, public databases, and a plethora of other sources to gather information. But its real power lies in the ability to connect disparate pieces of information, constructing a mosaic that reveals the bigger picture.

One of the fundamental aspects of OSINT is its versatility. It can be applied across various stages of a financial investigation, from the initial intelligence gathering to building a case for prosecution. OSINT techniques can unearth leads, corroborate evidence, and provide insights that would be challenging, if not impossible, to obtain through other means.

Navigating the OSINT landscape requires more than just technical acumen; it demands a strong ethical and legal compass. The abundance of information available online comes with the responsibility to respect privacy and adhere to legal standards. This chapter delves into the ethical considerations and legal frameworks that govern the use of OSINT in financial investigations, ensuring that investigators are equipped not just with the tools but also with the knowledge to use them responsibly.

The application of OSINT in financial investigations is as diverse as the types of financial crimes it helps to unravel. From tracking down the beneficiaries of fraudulent schemes to exposing the financial infrastructures supporting terrorism, OSINT has proven to be an invaluable asset. Through real-world case studies, this chapter illustrates the practical applications of

OSINT, offering insights into its effectiveness in various investigative scenarios.

As we peer into the future, the role of OSINT in financial investigations is set to expand further. The continuous evolution of technology promises new tools and methodologies to enhance the OSINT arsenal. However, this future also brings new challenges, as criminals adapt to the increasing scrutiny of their digital footprints.

In conclusion, this chapter is not just an exploration of OSINT; it's a guidebook for the modern financial investigator. It's an invitation to embark on a journey of discovery, where the vast expanse of publicly available information becomes a canvas, and OSINT tools are the brushes with which investigators paint a clearer picture of the financial crimes they seek to solve. As you turn the pages, you'll gain not just knowledge but also the perspective and skills to navigate the ever-evolving landscape of financial investigations in the digital age.

2.1 Understanding OSINT and its Value

Open Source Intelligence (OSINT) refers to the collection and analysis of information that is publicly available. In the context of financial investigations, OSINT can be a powerful tool for uncovering hidden assets, identifying financial connections, and developing leads.

The internet is a vast repository of publicly available information, including:

Social media profiles and posts: Individuals often share personal and professional information on social media platforms, which can reveal their connections, activities, and even their location.

Public records and databases: Government agencies, courts, and regulatory bodies maintain public records and databases containing information on individuals, businesses, and financial transactions.

Corporate filings and websites: Companies are required to disclose certain information publicly, such as their financial statements, ownership structure, and business activities.

News articles and media reports: News outlets and media sources often report on financial crimes and investigations, providing valuable insights and leads.

Online forums and discussion boards: Individuals may discuss financial matters and even illegal activities on online forums and discussion boards, leaving behind a digital trail.

The value of OSINT lies in its ability to provide investigators with a wealth of information without the need for intrusive or covert methods. By leveraging publicly available data, investigators can develop leads, corroborate evidence, and build a more complete picture of the case.

However, it is important to note that OSINT investigations also raise legal and ethical considerations. Investigators must ensure that they are collecting and using information in a way that complies with all applicable laws and regulations, including data privacy laws. Additionally, investigators must be mindful of the potential for misinformation and bias in open sources and take steps to verify the accuracy and reliability of the information they collect.

For example, investigators might use OSINT to identify the assets of a suspected fraudster. By searching public records and databases, they can uncover real estate holdings, vehicle registrations, and other assets that may be subject to seizure or forfeiture.

What are some of the ethical considerations that investigators should be mindful of when conducting OSINT investigations?

OSINT is a powerful tool for financial investigators, providing access to a vast amount of publicly available information. However, it is crucial to use OSINT responsibly and ethically, ensuring compliance with legal and regulatory requirements and verifying the accuracy and reliability of the information collected.

By leveraging OSINT effectively, investigators can gain valuable insights, develop leads, and build stronger cases against financial criminals.

2.2 Utilizing Search Engines and Social Media Platforms

Search engines and social media platforms are invaluable tools for conducting OSINT investigations. These platforms contain a vast amount of publicly available information that can be used to identify individuals, uncover financial connections, and develop leads.

Search Engines:

Mastering advanced search engine techniques is crucial for effective OSINT investigations. Investigators can use search operators, filters, and other techniques to refine their searches and locate relevant information. Some useful search engine techniques include:

- Using quotation marks to search for exact phrases.
- Using Boolean operators (AND, OR, NOT) to combine search terms.
- Filtering search results by date, location, or file type.
- Utilizing advanced search options offered by search engines.

Social Media Platforms:

Social media platforms are a treasure trove of information about individuals and organizations. Investigators can use social media to:

Identify individuals and their connections.

- Gather information about their activities and interests.
- Track their movements and locations.
- Uncover potential relationships and networks.
- Identify potential witnesses or informants.

However, it is important to note that social media investigations raise privacy concerns. Investigators must be aware of the legal and ethical implications of collecting information from social media platforms and ensure that they comply with all applicable laws and regulations.

For example, investigators might use social media to identify and locate a suspect in a financial crime. By analyzing the suspect's social media profiles and posts, investigators can gather information about their friends and associates, their places of employment, and their recent activities. This information can be used to develop leads and track down the suspect.

What are some of the challenges associated with conducting investigations on social media platforms?

Search engines and social media platforms are powerful tools for OSINT investigations, but it is important to use them responsibly and ethically. Investigators must be aware of the legal and privacy implications of collecting information from these sources and take steps to verify the accuracy and reliability of the information they find.

By mastering advanced search techniques and understanding the nuances of social media investigations, investigators can leverage these platforms to uncover valuable information and build stronger cases.

Here are some tips and tricks for investigators: Before delving into the investigative techniques discussed in this book, it's crucial to understand the concept of covert accounts, also known as "Sock Puppets." These are online profiles that do not reveal your real identity. Many social platforms, like Facebook and Instagram, now require users to log in before performing any searches. Using your actual account could compromise your anonymity as an investigator. Creating covert accounts on these networks is free and can be done with fake details, though some platforms like Google, Facebook, Twitter, Instagram, and Yahoo may impose stringent verification processes before allowing access.

Email: It's essential to have a "clean" email address for your covert accounts. Every social network mandates an email address during the registration process, and you should avoid using any personal email addresses you already have. Techniques discussed in later chapters about tracing the ownership of email addresses could be applied to your accounts, hence the importance of creating a new email solely for your covert operations.

Selecting the right email provider is crucial. I advise against using well-known providers like GMX, Proton Mail, Yahoo, Gmail, or MSN as they're common among spammers and thus subject to intense scrutiny. My recommendation is to opt for a free email account from Fastmail (https://ref.fm/u14547153), an established provider that stands out for a couple of reasons. Firstly, they're one of the few services that don't require an existing email address to sign up, ensuring no link between your covert and personal accounts. Secondly, they tend to fly under the radar of major platforms like Facebook and aren't heavily monitored for suspicious activities.

Fastmail offers unlimited free accounts with a 30-day trial period. It's advisable to select an email address ending in fastmail.us instead of the more commonly used fastmail.com during the account setup process. Once your new email is active, you can proceed with creating covert profiles. Be mindful that the free trial limits access to the email account after 30 days, making it potentially unsuitable for extended investigations. For longer-term needs, I maintain a paid account, which provides up to 250 permanent alias email addresses.

Facebook: Establishing a new account on Facebook poses significant challenges. Typically, Facebook mandates a cellular phone number for sending and verifying a text message during account creation. Unfortunately, VOIP numbers like those from Google Voice are no longer accepted. A viable workaround involves disabling any VPN, Tor Browser, or similar IP-concealing services and using a standard residential or business internet connection. Prior to account setup, ensure all internet cache is cleared, and you're logged out of existing accounts. Opt for registering via m.facebook.com, the mobile version of Facebook, which tends to be more lenient with new accounts. Use the newly created Fastmail email for registration, which should, in most cases, circumvent the need for a phone number verification. If this approach doesn't work, it may be due to specific factors related to your computer or internet connection. Persistence is key, and utilizing public library Wi-Fi can often yield success. For Instagram, which falls under Facebook's umbrella, expect a similar level of account creation rigor.

Twitter (X): While many Twitter-related techniques detailed later in the book don't necessitate an account, third-party tools do require you to be logged in. It's advisable to have a covert account ready. Typically, using a legitimate email address from a non-masked residential or business internet connection facilitates hassle-free account creation. While a VPN might sometimes be used for account creation, it's not consistently reliable.

Google/Gmail/Voice: Despite Google's heightened vigilance against questionable account registrations, success in setting up new accounts is still attainable. Similar to the strategies outlined before, attempts to create accounts via Tor or a VPN are generally thwarted by Google. Utilizing your Fastmail email as a secondary contact method during the sign-up process often meets Google's verification requirements. Additionally, initiating account creation using Google's Chrome browser, as opposed to a privacy-focused browser like Firefox, tends to encounter less resistance, likely because Chrome is a Google product.

Network Considerations: While my preference leans towards conducting online investigations with the anonymity provided by a VPN, this approach needs careful handling. Account creation via VPN can raise flags about your activities. Instead, opting for public Wi-Fi networks—found in libraries or cafés—usually faces less scrutiny. After establishing the account using public Wi-Fi, I transition to VPN use the following day. To avoid raising suspicions, I consistently use the same VPN provider and select a similar location for each session. This strategy helps establish a consistent usage pattern, enhancing the likelihood of uninterrupted access to the account.

Phone Verification: When online services detect any anomalies with your new account, they will invariably request a legitimate phone number for verification, rejecting landlines and VOIP numbers in favor of a genuine cellular number. To navigate this requirement, I utilize Mint Mobile SIM cards, which are readily available for purchase at a minimal cost on Amazon. Each card comes with a temporary phone number, equipped with a week-long trial period. I activate these SIMs using an older Android device, acquire a number, and subsequently employ it for registration across various platforms. Once the account is established, I promptly replace the cellular number with a VOIP alternative and enhance security with two-factor authentication (2FA).

Two-Factor Authentication (2FA): Post account creation, my immediate step is to enable two-factor authentication, adding an additional layer of security that typically involves a text message or a token generated by an app like Authy. This step is crucial as it signals to the service provider that there's a genuine user behind the account, reducing the likelihood of being mistaken for a malicious automated bot.

Maintaining Account Activity: To prevent the newly created account from being flagged or suspended, regular activity is key. An account that remains inactive for an extended period is prone to suspension upon re-entry. Conversely, periodic engagement, such as weekly logins, significantly diminishes the risk of account suspension, signaling ongoing and legitimate use.

It might seem convenient to utilize your personal social media accounts for investigative purposes, but this approach carries significant risks. While some platforms may not alert the person of interest about your investigative activities, others, particularly Facebook, might inadvertently signal your interest through mechanisms like friend suggestions. Moreover, the risk of mistakenly sending a friend request to a subject of interest is ever-present, which could compromise your investigation and professional integrity.

Given these potential pitfalls, it is prudent to abstain from using personal accounts for investigative work. Instead, maintaining several covert accounts is advisable, ensuring a clear separation between personal and professional online activities. While the intricacies of undercover operations are beyond this book's scope, it's essential to have access to valid, non-personal accounts to satisfy the login requirements of various social networks, thereby enabling effective online research without compromising your privacy or the investigation's integrity. With these covert accounts at your disposal, you are now equipped to delve into the realm of online investigations with enhanced security and anonymity.

Profile Enhancement for Covert Operations

While a sparse social network profile might be sufficient for investigative tasks, its emptiness can raise red flags for both the social network provider and the individual under scrutiny. Platforms like Facebook have a track record of deactivating profiles lacking in personal details. Moreover, individuals you are investigating might engage in their own open-source intelligence gathering on you once you commence your investigation.

In most cases, it's advisable to inject a modest amount of fabricated details into your covert profiles to avoid drawing undue attention. It's crucial, however, to ensure that these fabricated details have no ties to your real identity, encompassing aspects like hobbies, profession, or geographical location. To this end, I predominantly utilize content generated randomly or by artificial intelligence to flesh out these profiles.

For **images**, incorporating a profile picture can lend a degree of legitimacy to your covert account, potentially reducing the likelihood of the account being flagged by platforms like Facebook or Twitter as suspicious. A recommended resource is This Person Does Not Exist (thispersondoesnotexist.com), which employs AI to create realistic images of non-existent individuals. These images, unique and not duplicated elsewhere online, can be refreshed to generate different ones for various uses, ensuring you have a stockpile should the need arise or if the website becomes inaccessible.

Before proceeding, always align your actions with the needs of your investigation and adhere to any relevant policies set by your organization.

Creating a Convincing Alias and Backstory:

When setting up a covert profile, the challenge isn't just in selecting a plausible alias but in fleshing out the accompanying details that lend credibility to this new persona. Crafting a comprehensive background that includes elements such as a maiden name, date of birth, place of birth, zodiac sign, along with creating a unique username and password, not to mention aligning with a particular religion or political stance, requires careful consideration. Utilizing tools like ElfQrin (elfqrin.com/fakeid.php) and Fake Name Generator (fakenamegenerator.com) can streamline this process, instantly generating a multi-faceted identity.

Enhancing Credibility with a Resume:

To infuse your covert identity with additional authenticity, consider supplementing your profile with a resume. This step can be particularly effective if there's a chance your target might conduct their own investigation into your profile. A detailed resume, accessible online, reinforces the perception of your persona as a genuine individual.

Creating a Believable Physical Space:

To further enhance the realism of your covert identity, you might explore using This Rental Does Not Exist (thisrentaldoesnotexist.com). Leveraging AI technology similar to that of This Person Does Not Exist, this service generates fictitious but realistic-looking interior images of homes. Originally intended to simulate rental properties or Airbnb listings, these images can serve as convincing depictions of your alias's supposed living space, should you need to showcase "personal" photos in your profile.

2.3 Exploring Public Records and Databases

Public records and databases maintained by government agencies, courts, and regulatory bodies can provide a wealth of information for financial investigators. These records often contain details about individuals, businesses, financial transactions, and legal proceedings.

Some examples of valuable public records and databases include:

Corporate filings: Companies are required to file various documents with government agencies, such as articles of incorporation, financial statements, and annual reports. These documents can provide insights into a company's ownership structure, financial health, and business activities.

Property ownership records: Public records can reveal who owns real estate and other assets, which can be valuable information in asset tracing and recovery efforts.

Court records: Court records can provide information about lawsuits, judgments, and other legal proceedings involving individuals and businesses.

Tax records: Tax records can reveal income, assets, and financial transactions, which can be useful in financial investigations.

Regulatory filings: Many industries are subject to government regulations, and companies are required to file reports with regulatory agencies. These reports can contain valuable information about a company's operations and financial activities.

Investigators can access public records and databases through various means, including online portals, physical visits to government offices, and Freedom of Information Act (FOIA) requests. It is important to note that access to certain records may be restricted or require legal authorization.

For example, investigators might search public records to identify the assets of a suspected fraudster. By searching property ownership records, they can uncover real estate holdings, vehicle registrations, and other assets that may be subject to seizure or forfeiture.

What are some of the challenges associated with accessing and analyzing public records and databases?

Public records and databases are valuable resources for financial investigators, but it is important to be aware of the challenges associated with accessing and analyzing this information. Investigators must ensure that they have the legal authority to access certain records and must be able to navigate complex databases and interpret the information they find.

By effectively utilizing public records and databases, investigators can gain valuable insights, develop leads, and build stronger cases against financial criminals.

2.4 Extracting Information from Websites and Online Forums

Websites and online forums can be valuable sources of information for financial investigators. These platforms may contain information about individuals, businesses, financial transactions, and even discussions about illegal activities.

Investigators can use various techniques to extract information from websites and online forums, including:

Web scraping: This technique involves using automated tools to extract data from websites. Web scraping can be used to collect large amounts of data, such as financial data, product information, and customer reviews.

Website analysis: Investigators can analyze website traffic patterns, domain registration information, and other website data to identify connections and uncover hidden information.

Forum monitoring: Investigators can monitor online forums and discussion boards for relevant information and discussions about financial crimes or specific targets of investigations.

It is important to note that extracting information from websites and online forums must be done in compliance with the law and ethical guidelines. Investigators should be aware of the terms of service and privacy policies of the websites they are accessing and avoid any activities that could be considered hacking or unauthorized access.

For example, investigators might use web scraping to collect data from a website suspected of being involved in fraudulent activity. This data could then be analyzed to identify patterns and connections that could lead to the identification of the perpetrators.

What are some of the ethical considerations associated with extracting information from websites and online forums?

Extracting information from websites and online forums can be a valuable investigative technique, but it is important to do so ethically and responsibly. Investigators must ensure that they are not violating any laws or infringing on the privacy of individuals.

By using appropriate techniques and adhering to ethical guidelines, investigators can leverage websites and online forums to uncover valuable information and build stronger cases.

2.5 Verifying and Analyzing OSINT Data

Verifying and analyzing the information collected from open sources is crucial for ensuring the accuracy and reliability of OSINT findings. Investigators must critically evaluate the information they gather and take steps to confirm its authenticity and validity.

Some key steps in verifying and analyzing OSINT data include:

Source evaluation: Assess the credibility and reliability of the source of information. Consider the source's reputation, potential biases, and the context in which the information was published.

Cross-referencing: Verify information by comparing it with other sources and data points. Look for corroborating evidence and inconsistencies that may raise red flags.

Fact-checking: Utilize fact-checking tools and resources to verify the accuracy of information, especially when dealing with claims made on social media or online forums.

Data analysis: Use data analysis tools and techniques to identify patterns, connections, and anomalies in the collected data. This can help investigators develop leads and draw meaningful conclusions.

Critical thinking: Apply critical thinking skills to evaluate the information and avoid jumping to conclusions based on incomplete or unverified data.

It is important to document the verification process and maintain a record of the steps taken to confirm the accuracy and reliability of the information. This documentation can be crucial if the OSINT findings are used as evidence in legal proceedings.

For example, investigators might use cross-referencing to verify the identity of a suspect. They might compare the suspect's social media profiles with public records and other online sources to confirm their name, address, and other identifying information.

What are some of the challenges associated with verifying and analyzing OSINT data?

Verifying and analyzing OSINT data can be challenging due to the sheer volume of information available and the potential for misinformation and bias. Investigators must be critical thinkers and employ rigorous verification techniques to ensure the accuracy and reliability of their findings.

By implementing a systematic approach to verification and analysis, investigators can ensure that the OSINT data they collect is accurate, reliable, and admissible as evidence.

Chapter 3: Tracing the Money: Digital Payment Systems and Cryptocurrency Investigations

"Money is the root of all evil." - 1 Timothy 6:10

Welcome to Chapter 3, where we delve into the intricate world of digital payment systems and cryptocurrency, the new frontiers in financial transactions that have redefined the landscape of financial investigations. As the digital age forges ahead at an unprecedented pace, the financial industry has been at the forefront of embracing these technological advancements, offering both opportunities and challenges in the realm of financial investigations.

In this chapter, we navigate the complex web of digital payment systems, where traditional money trails blur into the virtual world, making the task of tracing financial activities more intricate yet fascinating. The rise of cryptocurrencies, with their promise of anonymity and decentralization, has further added layers of complexity, creating a parallel financial ecosystem that operates beyond the traditional banking sector.

Digital payment systems have revolutionized the way we transact, offering convenience and efficiency but also opening new avenues for financial crimes. From online banking to mobile wallets and peer-to-peer payment platforms, the digitalization of financial transactions has created a dynamic environment where investigators must be adept at navigating a multitude of channels through which money can flow.

This chapter provides a deep dive into the mechanisms of various digital payment systems, dissecting how they work, their role in the financial landscape, and their implications for financial investigations. By understanding the nuances of these systems, investigators can better trace the flow of illicit funds, identify patterns of fraudulent activities, and uncover the financial networks that underpin criminal enterprises.

Cryptocurrencies, once a niche interest, have burgeoned into a formidable force in the financial sector, presenting a unique set of challenges for financial investigators. The decentralized nature of cryptocurrencies, coupled with the anonymity they can provide, makes them attractive for illicit activities, from money laundering to financing terrorism.

In this chapter, we embark on an exploration of the cryptocurrency ecosystem, examining how cryptocurrencies operate, the infrastructure that supports them, and the challenges they pose in financial investigations. We delve into blockchain technology, the backbone of cryptocurrencies, to understand how it can be both a tool for anonymity and a record of transactions that, if deciphered, offers a wealth of information for investigators.

Navigating the digital landscape requires a new set of skills and strategies. This chapter equips you with the knowledge and tools to effectively investigate financial crimes in the digital realm. We explore advanced techniques for tracing digital transactions, from the use of blockchain analytics to unraveling the complexities of digital wallets.

The chapter also addresses the legal and ethical considerations that come with investigating digital financial activities. As the line between privacy and investigation blurs, it's imperative that investigators not only have the technical prowess but also a firm understanding of the legal frameworks that govern digital financial transactions.

As we delve into the future, it's clear that digital payment systems and cryptocurrencies will continue to evolve, bringing new challenges and opportunities for financial investigators. Staying ahead in this dynamic environment requires continuous learning and adaptation.

In this chapter, we provide a foundation for understanding the digital financial landscape, offering a blend of technical knowledge, investigative strategies, and legal insights. Whether you're a seasoned investigator or new to the field of financial investigations, this chapter is designed to empower you with the skills and knowledge to navigate the complex world of digital finance, ensuring you're prepared to tackle the financial crimes of today and tomorrow.

3.1 Understanding Digital Payment Systems

Digital payment systems have revolutionized the way we transact financially, offering convenience, speed, and accessibility. However, the digital nature of these transactions also presents challenges for financial investigators seeking to trace the flow of funds and identify illicit activities.

There are various types of digital payment systems, each with its own unique characteristics and data trails:

Online banking: Transactions conducted through online banking platforms leave behind digital records, including transaction logs, account statements, and IP addresses.

Mobile wallets: Mobile payment systems, such as Apple Pay and Google Pay, generate transaction data that can be accessed by investigators with proper authorization.

Payment processors: Third-party payment processors, such as PayPal and Stripe, facilitate online transactions and maintain records of these transactions.

Prepaid cards: Prepaid cards can be used to make purchases and transfer funds anonymously, making it difficult to trace the flow of funds.

Investigators need to understand the specific features and data trails associated with each type of digital payment system to effectively trace financial transactions and identify suspicious activities. This often involves obtaining transaction logs, account information, and other relevant data from financial institutions and payment processors.

However, tracing digital payments can be challenging, especially when transactions cross borders. Investigators may need to navigate complex legal and regulatory frameworks to obtain information from foreign jurisdictions. Additionally, the increasing use of anonymizing technologies and cryptocurrencies can further complicate tracing efforts.

For example, investigators might request transaction logs from a payment processor to trace the flow of funds in a suspected fraud case. By analyzing the transaction data, investigators can identify the parties involved, the amounts transferred, and the timing of the transactions. This information can be used to build a case and identify the perpetrators.

What are some of the challenges associated with tracing financial transactions through digital payment systems?

Tracing financial transactions through digital payment systems can be complex and challenging, especially when dealing with cross-border payments and anonymizing technologies. Investigators need to be familiar with the different types of digital payment systems and their data trails, as well as the legal and regulatory frameworks governing access to financial information.

By understanding the complexities of digital payment systems and employing appropriate investigative techniques, investigators can effectively trace the flow of funds and uncover financial crimes.

3.2 Demystifying Cryptocurrency

Cryptocurrency has emerged as a new frontier in financial transactions, offering a decentralized and pseudonymous way to transfer value. While cryptocurrency offers many legitimate uses, its unique characteristics also make it attractive for illicit activities, such as money laundering and fraud.

To effectively investigate financial crimes involving cryptocurrency, it is crucial to understand the underlying technology and its implications for tracing transactions.

Key Concepts:

Blockchain: Cryptocurrency transactions are recorded on a public, distributed ledger called a blockchain. This ledger is immutable, meaning that transactions cannot be altered or deleted.

Wallets: Cryptocurrency is stored in digital wallets, which are identified by unique alphanumeric addresses.

Exchanges: Cryptocurrency exchanges facilitate the buying, selling, and trading of cryptocurrencies.

Challenges for Investigators:

The pseudonymous nature of cryptocurrency transactions presents significant challenges for investigators. While transactions are recorded on the blockchain, the identities of the individuals behind the wallet addresses are often obscured.

This makes it difficult to trace the flow of funds and identify the parties involved in illicit activities.

Investigative Techniques:

Despite the challenges, investigators can employ various techniques to trace cryptocurrency transactions and identify individuals involved in financial crimes:

Blockchain analysis: Specialized tools and techniques can be used to analyze blockchain data and identify patterns, connections, and potential leads.

Exchange investigations: Investigators can work with cryptocurrency exchanges to obtain KYC/AML data and transaction records associated with specific wallets.

Wallet tracing: By analyzing blockchain data and transaction patterns, investigators can sometimes identify the individuals or entities behind specific wallets.

For example, investigators might use blockchain analysis to trace the flow of funds in a ransomware attack. By following the movement of cryptocurrency from the victim's wallet to the attacker's wallet, investigators can potentially identify the attacker and recover the stolen funds.

What are some of the challenges and opportunities associated with investigating financial crimes involving cryptocurrency?

Investigating financial crimes involving cryptocurrency presents unique challenges due to the pseudonymous nature of transactions and the decentralized nature of blockchain technology. However, by leveraging specialized tools and techniques, collaborating with cryptocurrency exchanges, and employing advanced investigative methods, investigators can trace cryptocurrency flows and identify individuals involved in illicit activities.

As cryptocurrency continues to evolve and become more mainstream, it is crucial for financial investigators to stay informed about the latest technologies and investigative techniques to effectively combat financial crime in this new frontier.

Hera are some tips and tricks fpr investigators: **Blockchain** (blockchain.info) is an invaluable resource for scrutinizing Bitcoin transactions. By inputting a Bitcoin address, users can access comprehensive data, including the number of transactions associated with that address, the total Bitcoin received in USD, the current balance, and a detailed record of all transactions. While this service might not reveal real-world identities directly, it offers profound insights into the financial activities of the address in question. For instance, an analysis could reveal that a particular account has received a total of

19.12688736 Bitcoin, valued at $287,391.14 USD at the time of analysis.

On the other hand, **Bitcoin Who's Who** (bitcoinwhoswho.com) provides an enhanced analytical perspective on Bitcoin addresses. It can identify if an address is linked to suspicious activities, such as ransomware operations, and if it has been mentioned across various media platforms. The service also offers information on transaction IP addresses, which, despite likely being masked by VPNs, adds an extra layer of data for investigators. While Blockchain serves as a robust tool for dissecting transaction details, Bitcoin Who's Who offers contextual insights, helping investigators understand the broader implications of the activity associated with a Bitcoin address.

BlockChair (blockchair.com) stands out as a versatile platform in the realm of cryptocurrency transactions, offering expansive coverage across various digital currencies. This service enables users to delve into the specifics of transactions for a wide array of cryptocurrencies beyond just Bitcoin. By navigating to specific URLs dedicated to each currency, users can effortlessly access detailed information such as balance and transaction history for any given address.

For example, to investigate a Bitcoin address, one would use the URL pattern https://blockchair.com/bitcoin/address/1EzwoHti

XB4iFwedPr49iywjZn2nnekhoj, where comprehensive transaction data is readily available. BlockChair's strength lies in its broad spectrum of supported currencies, including Ethereum, Ripple, Bitcoin Cash, Litecoin, Bitcoin SV, Dash, Dogecoin, and Groestlcoin.

Users can tailor their search to different cryptocurrencies by altering the URL structure, substituting "xxx" with the address they wish to investigate. This functionality allows for a seamless transition between different currency searches, offering a centralized platform for diverse cryptocurrency investigations. Whether you're examining a Bitcoin, Ripple, or Litecoin address, BlockChair provides a unified, user-friendly interface to access pivotal financial data across the cryptocurrency landscape.

Bitcoin Abuse (bitcoinabuse.com) serves a specialized purpose within the realm of virtual currency investigations. It acts as a centralized resource where users can discover if a specific cryptocurrency address has been flagged for involvement in illicit activities. This platform can be instrumental in providing context and background during investigations, especially when assessing the credibility and history of a virtual currency address.

For instance, by visiting a report page like https://www.bitcoinabuse.com/reports/1KUKcwCv64cXQZa4csaA1cF3PPTio6Yt2t, users gain access to detailed reports from individuals who have encountered malicious activities linked to the address. The platform chronicles various reports, offering insights such as the nature of the malicious activity (like sextortion or ransomware), associated dates, and even email addresses used in fraudulent schemes.

An example entry might detail incidents from September 21, 2019, categorizing the nature of the abuse (such as sextortion or claims of a hacked computer) and listing any involved email addresses that purportedly engaged in these activities. This level of detail furnishes investigators with a clearer understanding of the address's history, aiding in the construction of a comprehensive profile of its associated activities and potentially linking it to broader malicious campaigns.

3.3 Investigating Cryptocurrency Exchanges and Wallets

Cryptocurrency exchanges play a central role in the cryptocurrency ecosystem, facilitating the buying, selling, and trading of cryptocurrencies. They also serve as gateways between the cryptocurrency world and the traditional financial system, allowing users to convert cryptocurrencies to fiat currency and vice versa.

For financial investigators, cryptocurrency exchanges can be valuable sources of information and evidence. Exchanges typically collect KYC/AML (Know Your Customer/Anti-Money Laundering) data from their users, which can help identify individuals behind wallet addresses. Additionally, exchanges maintain records of transactions conducted on their platforms, which can be used to trace the flow of funds.

However, obtaining information from cryptocurrency exchanges can be challenging. Exchanges may be located in foreign jurisdictions with different legal and regulatory frameworks. Additionally, some exchanges may be reluctant to cooperate with investigators due to concerns about privacy and data security.

Investigative Strategies:

When investigating cryptocurrency exchanges and wallets, investigators can employ various strategies:

Legal requests: Investigators can use legal instruments, such as subpoenas and search warrants, to obtain information from exchanges. This may require cooperation with foreign authorities if the exchange is located outside the investigator's jurisdiction.

Collaboration with exchanges: Some exchanges may be willing to cooperate with investigators voluntarily, especially if they have robust AML/KYC procedures in place and are committed to combating financial crime.

Blockchain analysis: Investigators can analyze blockchain data to identify patterns and connections between wallets and exchanges. This can help trace the flow of funds and identify potential suspects.

For example, investigators might subpoena a cryptocurrency exchange to obtain KYC/AML data and transaction records associated with a wallet suspected of being used for money laundering. This information can help identify the individual behind the wallet and trace the flow of illicit funds.

What are some of the legal and regulatory challenges associated with investigating cryptocurrency exchanges?

Investigating cryptocurrency exchanges can be complex due to the global nature of the cryptocurrency market and the varying legal and regulatory frameworks across jurisdictions. Investigators need to navigate these complexities and ensure that they comply with all applicable laws and regulations when obtaining information from exchanges.

By understanding the legal and regulatory landscape and employing appropriate investigative strategies, investigators can effectively gather evidence from cryptocurrency exchanges and wallets to build strong cases against financial criminals.

3.4 Utilizing Blockchain Forensics

Blockchain forensics is a specialized field that involves the analysis of blockchain data to trace cryptocurrency transactions and identify illicit activities. Blockchain forensics tools and techniques can be used to:

Trace the flow of funds: Investigators can follow the movement of cryptocurrency from one wallet to another on the blockchain, creating a visual representation of the transaction history.

Identify wallet owners: While blockchain transactions are pseudonymous, blockchain forensics can sometimes help identify the individuals or entities behind specific wallets by analyzing transaction patterns and linking wallets to known entities.

Detect suspicious activities: Blockchain forensics tools can identify patterns and anomalies in transaction data that may indicate money laundering, fraud, or other illicit activities.

Cluster wallets: By analyzing transaction patterns and connections, investigators can group wallets together that are likely controlled by the same individual or entity.

Blockchain forensics is a powerful tool for investigating financial crimes involving cryptocurrency. However, it is important to note that blockchain forensics also has limitations:

Anonymity: While blockchain forensics can help identify wallet owners in some cases, many wallets remain anonymous, making it difficult to trace transactions back to real-world individuals.

Transaction mixing: Criminals can use mixing services to obscure the flow of funds, making it more difficult to trace transactions.

Cross-border transactions: Cryptocurrency transactions can easily cross borders, which can complicate investigations and require cooperation with foreign authorities.

For example, investigators might use blockchain forensics to trace the flow of funds in a ransomware attack. By analyzing the blockchain data, investigators can identify the wallet address used by the attacker to receive the ransom payment. This information can then be used to try to identify the attacker and recover the stolen funds.

What are some of the emerging trends in blockchain forensics?

Blockchain forensics is a rapidly evolving field, with new tools and techniques being developed to address the challenges associated with investigating cryptocurrency transactions. Some emerging trends include the use of artificial intelligence and machine learning to analyze blockchain data and the development of more sophisticated tools for deanonymizing wallets.

As blockchain technology continues to evolve, blockchain forensics will play an increasingly important role in financial investigations. By leveraging the latest tools and techniques, investigators can effectively trace cryptocurrency transactions, identify illicit activities, and bring financial criminals to justice.

3.5 Building a Cryptocurrency Investigation Strategy

Investigating financial crimes involving cryptocurrency requires a specialized approach and a deep understanding of blockchain technology and cryptocurrency markets. Building a comprehensive and effective investigation strategy is crucial for success in this complex and evolving field.

Key steps in building a cryptocurrency investigation strategy include:

Case assessment: Define the scope of the investigation, identify the specific cryptocurrency involved, and determine the desired outcome.

Collaboration with experts: Engage with cryptocurrency experts and blockchain forensic specialists to leverage their knowledge and expertise.

Blockchain analysis: Utilize blockchain forensics tools and techniques to trace the flow of funds, identify wallets, and detect suspicious activities.

Exchange investigations: If relevant, collaborate with cryptocurrency exchanges to obtain KYC/AML data and transaction records.

Legal considerations: Navigate the complex legal and regulatory landscape surrounding cryptocurrency investigations, including data privacy laws and international cooperation requirements.

Evidence collection and preservation: Implement strict chain of custody procedures to ensure the integrity and admissibility of digital evidence.

Contingency planning: Anticipate potential roadblocks and develop contingency plans to address challenges such as transaction mixing and anonymizing technologies.

Throughout the investigation, the strategy should be reviewed and updated regularly to reflect new information and developments. Flexibility and adaptability are crucial in cryptocurrency investigations, as the technology and criminal tactics are constantly evolving.

For example, in a case involving a suspected cryptocurrency Ponzi scheme, the investigation strategy might involve analyzing blockchain data to identify the wallets used by the perpetrators, tracing the flow of funds, and collaborating with cryptocurrency exchanges to obtain KYC/AML data. The strategy would also need to address legal considerations, such as obtaining warrants and ensuring the admissibility of evidence.

What are some of the unique challenges and considerations when building a cryptocurrency investigation strategy?

Building a cryptocurrency investigation strategy requires a deep understanding of blockchain technology, cryptocurrency markets, and the legal and regulatory landscape. Investigators must be prepared to address challenges such as anonymity, transaction mixing, and cross-border transactions.

By developing a comprehensive and adaptable strategy, collaborating with experts, and utilizing the latest investigative techniques, investigators can increase their chances of success in uncovering financial crimes involving cryptocurrency.

Cyber Threats: Terminology and Classification

Cybercrime encompasses illegal activities facilitated by the internet or other computer networks, including websites, chat rooms, and emails. The European Commission in 2007 categorized cybercrime into three sectors: conventional crimes conducted through cyber means, like fraud and forgery via online platforms; the dissemination of illegal content, such as child exploitation material; and offenses unique to the digital realm, such as hacking and denial of service (DoS) attacks. The Commission differentiates between 'true' cybercrimes, which are offenses that solely exist in cyberspace, like hacking, virus distribution, cyber-vandalism, and domain name hijacking, and 'e-enabled' crimes, which are traditional crimes that have adapted to the digital age, including credit card fraud, data theft, defamation, extortion, online pornography, hate speech, money laundering, copyright violation, and cyber-terrorism. This distinction highlights the penetration of criminal activities into the digital landscape, mirroring the broad spectrum of human behavior online.

Cyber-attacks are increasingly recognized as critical threats to national security, characterized by their capacity to disrupt legitimate network functions. These attacks can compromise network devices, overload systems, and deny service to authorized users. Attackers exploit vulnerabilities, such as software bugs and configuration errors, to hinder network operations. Their objective often involves conducting reconnaissance to gather information stealthily before launching a targeted assault. The element of "secrecy" plays a crucial role in organized cyber-attacks, with perpetrators using various methods to maintain anonymity, from utilizing public cyber-cafes to employing advanced techniques to obscure internet routing.

Cybercriminals leverage the anonymity provided by the internet to conduct illicit activities, including phishing, spamming, blackmail, identity theft, and drug trafficking. While network security tools are designed to detect vulnerabilities and collect data, they can be utilized by attackers to identify weaknesses and gather information essential for orchestrating successful attacks. Kshetri categorizes cyber-attacks into two primary types: targeted and opportunistic. Targeted attacks employ specific tools against predetermined targets, posing a greater threat than opportunistic attacks, which spread malware like worms and viruses broadly across the internet.

To combat the sophisticated nature of organized cybercrime, which often operates through untraceable accounts and compromised machines, it is vital to equip law enforcement agencies and national security entities with advanced tools. These tools are necessary for detecting, classifying, and defending against various forms of cyber-attacks, thereby enhancing the capability to thwart online criminal organizations.

Chapter 4: Unmasking the Actors: Identifying and Profiling Individuals and Organizations

"The man who wears a mask is never himself." - Victor Hugo

As we transition into Chapter 4, we delve into a critical aspect of financial investigations that transcends the traditional and digital realms alike—profiling. In an era where digital personas are as prevalent as physical identities, unmasking the actors behind financial schemes becomes a pivotal endeavor. This chapter is dedicated to the art and science of profiling, a process integral to illuminating the identities and uncovering the motivations of those involved in financial misconduct.

In the digital age, every interaction, transaction, and digital trail contributes to a person's or entity's digital persona. This chapter explores how investigators can harness this wealth of information to build comprehensive profiles.

These profiles are not mere collections of data but are intricate maps that guide us through the complex web of an individual's or organization's financial activities.

Profiling in financial investigations is an art form that requires a keen understanding of human behavior, technological acumen, and investigative intuition. Here, we explore methodologies for gathering data, analyzing patterns, and synthesizing information to create profiles that provide insights into the behaviors and motives of those engaged in financial crimes.

The chapter delves into the technological advancements that have transformed profiling in financial investigations. From data mining to advanced analytics, we explore the tools that enable investigators to sift through vast amounts of data to identify pertinent information. We also examine how social media, public records, and other open-source intelligence can be instrumental in constructing a profile.

With great power comes great responsibility. The chapter addresses the ethical considerations and legal boundaries that govern profiling in financial investigations. It is crucial to balance the pursuit of justice with respect for privacy and legal rights, ensuring that the investigative process upholds the highest ethical standards.

Through illustrative case studies, we demonstrate the application of profiling techniques in unraveling complex financial crimes. These real-world examples provide valuable insights into how profiles are constructed and utilized in various investigative contexts, showcasing the impact of effective profiling on the outcome of financial investigations.

As we look to the future, the chapter considers the evolving landscape of profiling in financial investigations. With the continuous advancement of technology and the increasing sophistication of financial crimes, the role of profiling will only grow in importance. We explore emerging trends and anticipate how investigators can adapt to stay ahead in this dynamic field.

In conclusion, Chapter 4 is not just an exploration of profiling techniques but a comprehensive guide to understanding the human element behind financial crimes. By mastering the art and science of profiling, investigators can uncover the motivations and tactics of individuals and entities, paving the way for more effective and impactful financial investigations.

4.1 Utilizing Online Data for Identification

In the digital age, individuals leave behind a vast amount of data online through their social media profiles, online interactions, and digital footprints. This data can be a valuable resource for financial investigators seeking to identify individuals involved in financial crimes.

Some of the ways online data can be used for identification include:

Social media profiles: Social media profiles often contain personal information, such as names, usernames, email addresses, phone numbers, and even physical addresses. Investigators can use this information to identify individuals and their connections.

Online aliases and usernames: Individuals may use aliases or usernames online, but investigators can sometimes link these aliases to real-world identities through cross-referencing and other investigative techniques.

IP addresses: IP addresses can be used to identify the location of a device used to access online accounts or conduct financial transactions.

Digital footprints: The websites individuals visit, the searches they conduct, and the online content they interact with can provide insights into their interests, activities, and potential involvement in financial crimes.

However, it is important to note that online data can be inaccurate, incomplete, or deliberately misleading. Investigators must take steps to verify the authenticity and reliability of online data before drawing conclusions or taking action. This may involve cross-referencing information with other sources, conducting additional research, and utilizing specialized tools and techniques.

For example, investigators might use social media profiles to identify individuals involved in a money laundering scheme. By analyzing the profiles of suspected participants, investigators can identify connections between individuals, uncover aliases, and gather evidence of their involvement in the scheme.

What are some of the challenges associated with using online data for identification?

Navigating the realm of online data for identification purposes presents a complex set of challenges, particularly in the context of financial investigations. The digital landscape offers a vast reservoir of information, yet its reliability and accuracy are often in question due to the ease with which identities can be masked or fabricated online.

Individuals with the intent to deceive or hide their real identities can easily adopt pseudonyms, construct entirely fictitious online personas, or distort digital information. These practices pose significant obstacles for investigators who rely on online data to pinpoint and understand the actors involved in financial misconduct or criminal activities.

The fluidity of online identities means that an investigator must approach each piece of digital data with a critical eye. Verification becomes a cornerstone of the investigative process. It's not enough to simply gather data; each piece must be cross-referenced and corroborated with additional sources to build a coherent and reliable picture of an individual's identity.

Moreover, the sheer volume of online data can be overwhelming. Investigators are often required to sift through vast quantities of information, discerning what is relevant and distinguishing between authentic data and digital chaff. This necessitates not only a keen sense of discernment but also the use of sophisticated digital tools and methodologies designed to filter and analyze large datasets effectively.

The dynamic and evolving nature of the internet adds another layer of complexity. Digital footprints can be ephemeral, with data changing or disappearing, and online platforms constantly updating their interfaces and privacy policies. This fluid environment demands agility and continuous learning from investigators to stay abreast of new technologies and methodologies for data extraction and analysis.

In the realm of financial investigations, the stakes are high. The ability to accurately identify individuals behind online data can unravel complex financial schemes, expose fraudulent activities, and hold perpetrators accountable. As such, investigators must navigate the intricacies of online data with a balanced approach that combines technical prowess with a stringent ethical framework.

This ethical framework is crucial as it underscores the respect for privacy and the legal boundaries within which investigators must operate. The pursuit of accuracy in identification should not infringe upon individual privacy rights nor overstep legal constraints, ensuring that the investigation maintains its integrity and the evidence collected is admissible in a court of law.

In conclusion, while the digital age provides investigators with unprecedented access to data that can be instrumental in identifying individuals involved in financial crimes, it also presents a unique set of challenges. These challenges require a comprehensive approach that includes critical evaluation, rigorous verification, ethical consideration, and a commitment to continuous learning and adaptation to new digital realities. Through such a multifaceted approach, investigators can effectively leverage online data, turning it into a powerful ally in the quest to uncover and combat financial crimes.

4.2 Investigating Corporate Structures and Ownership

Financial crimes often involve complex corporate structures and ownership arrangements designed to conceal the true identities of the individuals behind the activities. Investigators need to be able to pierce through these layers of complexity to identify the beneficial owners and key players involved.

Investigating corporate structures and ownership involves:

Gathering corporate filings: Companies are required to file various documents with government agencies, such as articles of incorporation, financial statements, and annual reports. These documents can provide information about the company's ownership structure, directors, and officers.

Analyzing ownership chains: Investigators may need to follow complex ownership chains to identify the ultimate beneficial owners of a company. This may involve tracing ownership through multiple layers of holding companies and subsidiaries, often located in different jurisdictions.

Identifying shell companies: Shell companies are often used to conceal the true ownership of assets and financial transactions. Investigators need to be able to identify shell companies and determine who is behind them.

Utilizing commercial databases: Commercial databases can provide information about companies, their ownership structures, and their directors and officers. These databases can be valuable resources for investigators seeking to unravel complex corporate structures.

Investigating corporate structures and ownership can be a complex and time-consuming process, especially when dealing with multinational corporations and offshore jurisdictions. Investigators may need to collaborate with foreign authorities and utilize specialized tools and techniques to pierce through layers of secrecy and identify the true beneficiaries of financial crimes.

For example, investigators might investigate a complex network of shell companies to uncover a money laundering scheme. By analyzing corporate filings, ownership chains, and financial transactions, investigators can identify the individuals who are ultimately controlling the shell companies and benefiting from the illicit activities.

What are some of the challenges associated with investigating corporate structures and ownership?

Investigating corporate structures and ownership stands as a formidable task in the realm of financial investigations. The intricate web of corporate entities, often designed with layers of complexity and sometimes intended obfuscation, poses significant hurdles for investigators aiming to uncover the true nature of business dealings and ownership.

Corporate entities can be structured in ways that intentionally mask the true ownership, using a variety of legal and financial mechanisms. One common tactic is the use of offshore jurisdictions, which often provide a veil of secrecy due to their lax reporting requirements and strong privacy laws. This can make it exceedingly difficult to trace the flow of funds or identify the ultimate beneficiaries of corporate transactions.

Moreover, the utilization of shell companies compounds the complexity. These entities, which typically have no active business operations, can be used as vehicles for various financial maneuvers, including tax evasion, money laundering, and hiding assets from creditors or legal scrutiny. They serve as a facade, behind which the real actors operate, making the task of identifying the true owners or controllers exceedingly challenging.

This investigative process is not only time-consuming but also demands significant resources. It often involves sifting through vast amounts of data, requiring a high level of expertise and sophisticated tools. Investigators need to have a deep understanding of corporate law, finance, and international business practices to effectively navigate this labyrinth.

Collaboration with experts in various fields is often essential to untangle complex corporate structures. Legal professionals, forensic accountants, and specialists in offshore jurisdictions can provide the necessary insight and expertise to make sense of convoluted corporate arrangements. This multidisciplinary approach is crucial in identifying weak points and potential leads within the corporate structure.

Leveraging commercial databases is another key strategy in these investigations. These databases can provide valuable information on corporate entities, including their registration details, financial filings, and associated individuals. However, the effectiveness of this approach is contingent on the quality and comprehensiveness of the database, as well as the investigator's ability to interpret and connect the information within a broader investigative context.

Despite these tools and strategies, the ever-evolving nature of corporate structures presents a moving target for investigators. Companies may frequently restructure, change jurisdictions, or alter their ownership arrangements, necessitating constant vigilance and adaptability from investigators.

Moreover, the international scope of modern corporations introduces additional layers of complexity. Different countries have varying levels of transparency and cooperation when it comes to sharing corporate data, and legal hurdles can impede cross-border investigations.

Navigating this global landscape requires not only expertise in domestic law but also an understanding of international legal frameworks and cooperation mechanisms.

In conclusion, investigating corporate structures and ownership is a daunting task fraught with obstacles. It demands a high level of skill, an interdisciplinary approach, and a thorough understanding of international business practices. Despite these challenges, with the right techniques and collaborations, investigators can peel back the layers of corporate complexity to expose the truth and hold entities accountable for their financial actions. This meticulous unraveling of corporate structures is not just a technical exercise but a crucial endeavor in upholding transparency, accountability, and justice in the business world.

4.3 Leveraging Network Analysis and Link Charts

Network analysis is a powerful technique used in financial investigations to visualize and analyze relationships between individuals, organizations, and financial transactions. By creating link charts, investigators can gain a clearer understanding of complex networks and identify key players, influencers, and potential co-conspirators.

Network analysis involves:

Identifying entities: This includes individuals, organizations, bank accounts, and other relevant entities involved in the financial crime.

Mapping connections: Investigators then map the connections between these entities, such as financial transactions, business relationships, and personal connections.

Visualizing the network: Using specialized software, investigators can create link charts that visually represent the network of entities and their connections.

Analyzing the network: Investigators can then analyze the network to identify key players, influencers, and potential co-conspirators. They can also identify patterns and anomalies that may indicate fraudulent activity.

Link charts can be valuable tools for presenting complex information in a clear and concise manner. They can help investigators identify hidden connections and relationships that might not be immediately apparent from traditional investigative methods.

For example, investigators might use network analysis to investigate a suspected Ponzi scheme. By creating a link chart of the individuals involved and their financial transactions, investigators can identify the key players in the scheme and how they are connected to each other.

This information can be used to build a case and identify potential victims.

What are some of the benefits and limitations of using network analysis and link charts in financial investigations?

Network analysis and link charts can be powerful tools for visualizing and analyzing complex networks, but they also have limitations. Investigators need to be careful not to draw conclusions based solely on network analysis, as correlation does not necessarily equal causation. Additionally, network analysis can be time-consuming and resource-intensive, and it may not be suitable for all investigations.

By using network analysis and link charts effectively, investigators can gain valuable insights into complex financial crimes and identify key players and networks involved. However, it is important to use these tools in conjunction with other investigative methods and to interpret the findings carefully.

4.4 Understanding Behavioral Patterns and Motivations

Understanding the behavioral patterns and motivations of individuals and organizations involved in financial crimes can be crucial for investigators. By analyzing behavior and motives, investigators can develop leads, predict future actions, and build stronger cases.

Some key aspects of behavioral analysis in financial investigations include:

Identifying red flags: Certain behaviors and activities can be indicative of fraudulent intent or financial crime. Investigators need to be aware of these red flags and investigate them further.

Analyzing financial transactions: Unusual or suspicious financial transactions can provide insights into the motives and activities of individuals and organizations.

Understanding psychological motivations: Greed, desperation, and other psychological factors can motivate individuals to commit financial crimes. Investigators can use psychological profiling techniques to understand the motivations of suspects.

Examining past behavior: Past financial crimes or misconduct can be indicative of future behavior. Investigators should examine the past behavior of individuals and organizations to identify potential risks and patterns.

Data analytics can also be used to identify behavioral patterns and anomalies. By analyzing large datasets of financial transactions, communications, and online activity, investigators can identify suspicious patterns that may warrant further investigation.

For example, investigators might analyze the financial transactions of a suspected fraudster to identify patterns of unusual spending or transfers to offshore accounts. This information can provide insights into the suspect's motives and help investigators build a case.

What are some of the challenges associated with understanding behavioral patterns and motivations in financial investigations?

Understanding human behavior and motivations can be complex and challenging. Individuals may have hidden motives or engage in deceptive behavior to conceal their true intentions. Additionally, financial crimes can be driven by a variety of factors, making it difficult to pinpoint the exact motivations behind specific actions.

By utilizing a combination of investigative techniques, data analytics, and psychological profiling, investigators can gain a deeper understanding of the behavioral patterns and motivations of individuals and organizations involved in financial crimes. This understanding can be crucial for developing leads, predicting future actions, and building strong cases.

4.5 Building Comprehensive Profiles

Building comprehensive profiles of individuals and organizations involved in financial crimes is essential for investigators. These profiles can help assess risk, predict future behavior, and develop effective investigative strategies.

Building a comprehensive profile involves integrating information from various sources, including:

Online data: Social media profiles, online interactions, and digital footprints can provide valuable insights into an individual's activities, connections, and potential involvement in financial crimes.

Public records and databases: Corporate filings, property ownership records, court records, and other public records can provide information about an individual's or organization's financial history, legal issues, and business activities.

Financial records: Bank statements, credit card records, and other financial documents can reveal patterns of spending, income sources, and potential fraudulent transactions.

Interviews and witness statements: Interviews with individuals who know the suspect or have information about their activities can provide valuable insights into their character, motivations, and potential involvement in financial crimes.

By integrating information from these various sources, investigators can develop a more complete picture of the individual or organization and their potential involvement in financial crimes. This information can then be used to assess risk, predict future behavior, and develop effective investigative strategies.

However, it is important to note that profiling can be subject to biases and ethical considerations. Investigators must be careful to avoid making assumptions or drawing conclusions based on stereotypes or incomplete information. It is crucial to rely on verified facts and evidence when building profiles and to use this information responsibly and ethically.

For example, investigators might build a comprehensive profile of a suspected fraudster by analyzing their social media activity, financial records, and past legal issues. This information can help investigators understand the suspect's motivations, identify potential co-conspirators, and develop strategies to apprehend them.

What are some of the ethical considerations associated with building profiles of individuals and organizations?

Building profiles of individuals and organizations can raise ethical concerns, particularly regarding privacy and potential biases. Investigators must ensure that they are collecting and using information in a responsible and ethical manner, complying with all applicable laws and regulations. Additionally, investigators must be aware of the potential for biases and stereotypes to influence their profiling efforts and take steps to mitigate these biases.

By using a comprehensive and ethical approach to profiling, investigators can gain valuable insights into the individuals and organizations involved in financial crimes and develop effective strategies to combat these crimes.

Chapter 5: Diving Deeper: Utilizing Advanced Investigative Techniques

"The deeper you dig, the more you find." - Unknown

Chapter 5 invites you into the sophisticated world of advanced investigative techniques that are pivotal in dissecting the anatomy of financial crimes in our increasingly digitalized landscape. This chapter is a deep dive into the complex yet fascinating realm of financial forensics, where each investigative method unveils a layer, revealing the intricate web woven by financial criminals.

The financial investigative landscape is akin to a vast ocean, where beneath the calm surface lies a world teeming with activity, much of it hidden from the naked eye. Here, we navigate the depths, employing advanced investigative techniques to illuminate the dark recesses where financial malfeasance lurks. This chapter is your compass in this journey, guiding you through the sophisticated methods that peel back layers, revealing the truths buried in complex data and deceptive practices.

Financial crimes have evolved, becoming more intricate and concealed beneath layers of digital complexity. To combat this, investigators must be equipped with a repertoire of advanced techniques. This chapter elucidates these methods, from data mining and analytics, which sift through mountains of information to unearth anomalies, to digital forensics that trace the faintest of digital footprints left by perpetrators.

In an era where technology intertwines with every aspect of life, financial investigations have embraced technological advancements to enhance their efficacy. We explore how cutting-edge technology, including artificial intelligence and machine learning, is being harnessed to predict, detect, and dissect financial crimes, offering investigators unprecedented insights into the mechanics of illicit financial schemes.

Understanding the application of these advanced techniques in real-world scenarios is crucial. Through detailed case studies, this chapter demonstrates how these methods are applied in actual investigations, providing a pragmatic perspective on the theoretical knowledge presented. These narratives showcase the triumphs, challenges, and the indispensable role of advanced investigative techniques in solving complex financial crimes.

With great power comes great responsibility. As we delve into these advanced techniques, the chapter also underscores the importance of ethical considerations and legal frameworks that guide financial investigations. It emphasizes the need for investigators to navigate this landscape with integrity, ensuring that their pursuit of truth does not infringe on privacy or civil liberties.

The final segment of the chapter casts an eye toward the future, contemplating the evolution of financial investigations as they adapt to the ever-changing landscape of financial crime. It encourages investigators to remain lifelong learners, continuously updating their arsenal of skills to stay ahead in this perpetual game of cat and mouse.

In essence, Chapter 5 is not just an exploration of advanced investigative techniques; it's a blueprint for the future of financial investigations. It equips you with the knowledge and insights to delve beyond the surface, unraveling the complexities of financial crimes to uphold justice and integrity in the financial world.

5.1 Utilizing Data Mining and Analytics

Data mining and analytics play an increasingly important role in modern financial investigations. With the vast amount of digital data available, investigators can leverage these techniques to identify patterns, anomalies, and hidden connections that may indicate fraudulent activity.

Data mining involves extracting useful information from large datasets. In financial investigations, data mining can be used to:

Identify suspicious transactions: By analyzing large datasets of financial transactions, data mining algorithms can identify transactions that deviate from the norm or exhibit patterns associated with fraud.

Detect anomalies: Data mining can help investigators identify unusual patterns in financial data, such as sudden spikes in spending or unexplained transfers of funds.

Uncover hidden connections: Data mining can reveal connections between individuals, organizations, and financial transactions that might not be immediately apparent.

Data analytics involves the analysis and interpretation of data to extract meaningful insights. In financial investigations, data analytics can be used to:

Understand complex financial networks: By analyzing financial transactions and relationships, investigators can gain a deeper understanding of complex financial networks and identify key players and influencers.

Predict future behavior: Data analytics can be used to identify patterns and trends that may indicate future fraudulent activity, allowing investigators to take proactive measures.

Build stronger cases: By providing insights and evidence, data analytics can help investigators build stronger cases against financial criminals.

Various data mining and analytics tools and techniques are available to investigators, including:

Statistical analysis: Statistical methods can be used to identify outliers and anomalies in financial data.

Machine learning: Machine learning algorithms can be trained to identify patterns and predict future behavior based on historical data.

Artificial intelligence: AI-powered tools can analyze vast amounts of data and identify complex patterns and connections that may be missed by human investigators.

For example, investigators might use data mining to analyze a large dataset of credit card transactions to identify potential fraudulent activity. The data mining algorithm could identify transactions that are outside the normal spending patterns of the cardholder or that originate from suspicious locations.

What are some of the challenges associated with using data mining and analytics in financial investigations?

Data mining and analytics are indispensable in the modern landscape of financial investigations, offering deep insights into vast datasets and unveiling patterns that may indicate fraudulent activities. However, the deployment of these technologies is fraught with challenges that can affect the outcomes of investigations.

Data Quality and Integrity

One of the primary concerns in using data mining and analytics is the quality and integrity of the data. Financial datasets are often massive and can be riddled with inaccuracies, inconsistencies, or missing values. The adage "garbage in, garbage out" is particularly relevant here; flawed data can lead to misleading analysis results, potentially directing investigators down incorrect paths. Ensuring data accuracy involves rigorous validation and cleaning processes, which can be resource-intensive but are crucial for reliable analysis.

Complexity of Tools and Techniques

The tools and techniques used in data mining and analytics are inherently complex and often require specialized knowledge to deploy effectively. Financial investigators must have a deep understanding of the methodologies and the ability to interpret the results accurately. This necessitates continuous training and development, as the field is rapidly evolving with new tools and techniques constantly emerging.

Algorithmic Bias and Interpretation

Another significant challenge is the potential for bias in algorithms and the interpretation of analytical results. Biases can be introduced in various stages, from data collection and preparation to the choice of algorithms and parameters. These biases can skew results, leading to incorrect conclusions or overlooking crucial information. Moreover, the interpretation of results from data mining and analytics requires a nuanced understanding of both the techniques used and the context of the investigation. Misinterpretation can result in missed opportunities to detect malfeasance or, conversely, the wrongful implication of individuals or entities.

Volume and Velocity of Data

The sheer volume of data that financial investigators have to sift through presents another hurdle. With the proliferation of digital financial transactions, the amount of data generated is enormous and continuously growing. Furthermore, the velocity at which new data is created and needs to be analyzed can overwhelm investigative teams. This necessitates the use of advanced data management and analysis techniques, which can be resource-intensive to implement and maintain.

Ethical and Legal Considerations

The use of data mining and analytics in financial investigations also raises ethical and legal considerations. The right to privacy and data protection laws must be balanced against the need for investigative thoroughness. Investigators must navigate these legal and ethical landscapes diligently, ensuring that their methods comply with all relevant statutes and norms.

Interdisciplinary Collaboration

Effectively addressing the challenges of data mining and analytics often requires interdisciplinary collaboration. Financial investigators may need to work closely with data scientists, legal experts, and industry specialists to ensure that their analyses are accurate, relevant, and compliant with legal standards. This collaboration can be challenging to coordinate but is essential for conducting robust and comprehensive financial investigations.

Future Proofing Skills and Tools

Finally, the rapidly evolving nature of technology means that tools and techniques can quickly become outdated. Investigators must stay abreast of developments in the field, continually updating their skills and the tools they use. This requires a commitment to ongoing learning and adaptability, which can be challenging in the face of daily investigative demands.

In conclusion, while data mining and analytics hold immense potential for unveiling financial fraud and misconduct, the challenges they present are substantial. Addressing these challenges requires a multifaceted approach, combining rigorous data management, specialized expertise, interdisciplinary collaboration, and a keen awareness of ethical and legal constraints.

5.2 Mastering Digital Forensics

Digital forensics is a crucial aspect of many financial investigations. It involves the recovery, preservation, and analysis of digital evidence from computers, mobile devices, and other digital storage media. Digital forensic techniques can be used to:

Recover deleted data: Even data that has been deleted from a device can often be recovered using specialized digital forensic tools.

Crack passwords: Digital forensic tools can be used to crack passwords and gain access to encrypted data.

Analyze file systems: Investigators can analyze file systems to identify hidden files, track file access times, and reconstruct user activity.

Extract metadata: Metadata associated with digital files can provide valuable information, such as the date and time a file was created or modified, and the identity of the user who created it.

Build timelines: Digital forensic investigators can build timelines of user activity based on the digital evidence they collect. This can help reconstruct events and identify potential suspects.

It is crucial to follow strict chain of custody procedures when handling digital evidence to ensure its integrity and admissibility in court. This involves documenting the collection, handling, and transfer of evidence to maintain a clear and verifiable record.

For example, investigators might conduct digital forensics on a suspect's computer to identify evidence of financial crime. This could involve recovering deleted files, analyzing internet browsing history, and extracting metadata from financial documents.

What are some of the challenges associated with digital forensics in financial investigations?

Digital forensics stands as a cornerstone in the investigation of financial crimes, offering a window into the digital actions of individuals and entities. However, the field is laden with complexities and challenges that necessitate a high degree of expertise and meticulous attention to detail from investigators.

Navigating a Diverse Digital Landscape

One of the primary challenges in digital forensics is the diversity of digital devices and file systems. Investigators must be proficient in dealing with various operating systems, mobile devices, cloud storage solutions, and even emerging technologies that could store pertinent data. This diversity requires a broad knowledge base and continuous learning to stay abreast of new technological developments.

Staying Ahead of Evolving Technologies

The rapid pace at which technology evolves adds another layer of complexity. Forensic tools and techniques that are effective today may become obsolete tomorrow as new devices and technologies emerge. Investigators must constantly update their knowledge and tools to stay effective in their role, necessitating a commitment to ongoing education and adaptation.

Deciphering Encrypted and Anonymized Data

The increasing use of encryption and anonymizing technologies poses a significant hurdle in digital investigations. Perpetrators often use these technologies to obscure their activities, making it challenging for investigators to access and interpret the data. While these technologies are formidable, advanced forensic tools and techniques can sometimes penetrate these defenses, though this often requires considerable time and resources.

Maintaining Chain of Custody

Adherence to strict chain of custody procedures is paramount in digital forensics. The integrity of digital evidence must be maintained from collection through analysis to presentation in court. Any lapse in these procedures can compromise the evidence, potentially rendering it inadmissible in legal proceedings. This necessitates rigorous documentation and secure handling practices to preserve the evidence's integrity.

Interdisciplinary Collaboration and Expertise

Effective digital forensics often requires collaboration across various disciplines. Investigators may need to work closely with cybersecurity experts, legal professionals, and industry specialists to interpret data correctly and contextualize it within the framework of the investigation. This interdisciplinary approach can be complex but is crucial for a comprehensive understanding of the digital evidence.

Legal and Ethical Considerations

Navigating the legal and ethical dimensions of digital forensics is essential. Investigators must ensure their methods comply with relevant laws and respect privacy rights, balancing the need for thorough investigation with respect for individual liberties. This balance is delicate and requires a deep understanding of legal frameworks and ethical norms.

Addressing Resource and Time Constraints

Digital forensic investigations can be resource-intensive and time-consuming, often requiring specialized equipment and software.

Investigators must manage these resources effectively, prioritizing tasks and deploying tools strategically to maximize efficiency without compromising thoroughness.

In conclusion, digital forensics is an intricate field that plays a crucial role in the investigation of financial crimes. Despite its challenges, it offers powerful means to uncover illicit activities and gather evidence.

By mastering a diverse array of technologies, adhering to rigorous procedures, and navigating legal and ethical landscapes, digital forensic investigators can uncover crucial insights that contribute to the resolution of complex financial crimes, ensuring accountability and justice in the digital age.

5.3 Conducting Covert Online Investigations

In some cases, financial investigators may need to conduct covert online investigations to gather evidence and identify suspects. This may involve using undercover online personas to infiltrate criminal networks or engage in online surveillance and monitoring.

Covert online investigations raise significant legal and ethical considerations. Investigators must ensure that their actions comply with all applicable laws and regulations, including those related to privacy and data protection.

Additionally, investigators must be mindful of the potential for entrapment and ensure that their actions do not induce individuals to commit crimes they would not otherwise commit.

Some common techniques used in covert online investigations include:

Creating undercover online personas: Investigators may create fake online profiles and personas to interact with suspects and gain access to criminal networks.

Online surveillance and monitoring: Investigators may use specialized software and tools to monitor online activity, such as chat rooms, forums, and social media platforms.

Electronic surveillance: In some cases, investigators may obtain legal authorization to conduct electronic surveillance, such as intercepting communications or monitoring internet activity.

It is crucial to note that covert online investigations should only be conducted by trained and experienced investigators with proper legal authorization. These investigations can be complex and sensitive, and it is essential to ensure that they are conducted in a lawful and ethical manner.

For example, investigators might create an undercover online persona to infiltrate a dark web marketplace suspected of facilitating the sale of stolen financial information. The undercover investigator could then gather evidence of the illegal activities and identify the individuals involved.

What are some of the ethical considerations associated with conducting covert online investigations?

Covert online investigations raise significant ethical concerns, particularly regarding privacy and the potential for entrapment. Investigators must ensure that their actions are proportionate, justified, and comply with all applicable laws and regulations. Additionally, investigators must be mindful of the potential impact on innocent individuals who may be caught up in the investigation.

By conducting covert online investigations in a responsible and ethical manner, investigators can gather valuable evidence and identify perpetrators of financial crimes while protecting the privacy and rights of individuals.

5.4 Leveraging Social Engineering Techniques

Social engineering involves manipulating individuals into divulging confidential information or taking actions that compromise their security. While social engineering techniques are often used by criminals to commit financial crimes, investigators can also leverage these techniques in a controlled and ethical manner to gather evidence and identify suspects.

Some common social engineering techniques used in investigations include:

Pretexting: Creating a false scenario to gain the trust of a target and elicit information. For example, an investigator might pose as a customer service representative to obtain account information from a suspect.

Phishing: Sending emails or messages that appear to be from legitimate sources to trick individuals into revealing confidential information or clicking on malicious links. Investigators might use phishing techniques to gain access to a suspect's online accounts or devices.

Baiting: Offering something of value to entice a target to take an action that compromises their security. For example, an investigator might offer a free download of software that contains a hidden tracking mechanism.

It is crucial to emphasize that social engineering techniques should only be used by trained and experienced investigators with proper legal authorization. These techniques can be highly manipulative and can have serious consequences for the individuals targeted. Investigators must ensure that their actions are proportionate, justified, and comply with all applicable laws and regulations.

For example, investigators might use social engineering techniques to obtain information from a suspect who is unwilling to cooperate. An investigator might pose as a potential business partner to gain the suspect's trust and elicit incriminating information.

What are some of the ethical considerations associated with using social engineering techniques in investigations?

Social engineering techniques can be highly manipulative and can have a significant impact on the individuals targeted. Investigators must carefully consider the potential risks and benefits before using these techniques and ensure that their actions are ethical and justified. Additionally, investigators must be transparent about their use of social engineering techniques and obtain informed consent from the individuals targeted whenever possible.

By using social engineering techniques responsibly and ethically, investigators can gather valuable evidence and identify perpetrators of financial crimes while minimizing the potential harm to individuals.

5.5 Integrating Advanced Techniques into Investigations

Advanced investigative techniques, such as data mining, digital forensics, and social engineering, can significantly enhance the effectiveness of financial investigations. However, it is crucial to integrate these techniques into a comprehensive investigation strategy to maximize their impact.

Effective integration involves:

Collaboration with experts: Investigators should collaborate with experts in data analytics, digital forensics, and social engineering to leverage their specialized knowledge and skills.

Tailoring the approach: The specific techniques used should be tailored to the nature of the crime, the available evidence, and the investigative objectives.

Prioritizing tasks: Advanced techniques can be time-consuming and resource-intensive. Investigators need to prioritize tasks and allocate resources effectively.

Maintaining chain of custody: It is crucial to maintain chain of custody for all evidence collected, including digital evidence obtained through advanced techniques.

Legal and ethical considerations: Investigators must ensure that their use of advanced techniques complies with all applicable laws and regulations and adheres to ethical guidelines.

For example, in a complex financial fraud investigation, investigators might utilize a combination of data mining to identify suspicious transactions, digital forensics to recover deleted data from computers and mobile devices, and social engineering techniques to elicit information from uncooperative suspects. By integrating these techniques into a comprehensive strategy, investigators can increase their chances of uncovering the full scope of the fraud and identifying the perpetrators.

What are some of the challenges associated with integrating advanced techniques into financial investigations?

Integrating advanced techniques into financial investigations can be challenging due to the complexity of these techniques and the need for specialized expertise. Additionally, investigators need to ensure that their use of these techniques complies with legal and ethical requirements.

By collaborating with experts, carefully planning the investigation strategy, and prioritizing tasks, investigators can effectively integrate advanced techniques into financial investigations and achieve successful outcomes.

As technology and criminal tactics continue to evolve, it is crucial for financial investigators to stay informed about the latest advancements in investigative techniques and adapt their strategies accordingly. By embracing new technologies and approaches, investigators can stay ahead of the curve and effectively combat financial crime in the digital age.

Chapter 6: Navigating the Legal Landscape: Data Privacy, Regulations, and International Cooperation

"Law is order, and good law is good order." - Aristotle

Welcome to Chapter 6, a pivotal section that serves as the legal compass for financial investigators steering through the complex waters of international law and data privacy. As the digital age expands the frontiers of financial investigations beyond borders, understanding the legal frameworks and cooperative mechanisms becomes indispensable. This chapter demystifies the intricate interplay between law, ethics, and financial forensics, providing investigators with the essential knowledge to conduct their inquiries within the bounds of legality and mutual respect for sovereignty.

Financial crimes are no longer confined by geographical boundaries; they span across nations, weaving a tangled web that only international cooperation and adherence to legal protocols can unravel. Here, we dissect the legal codes, treaties, and agreements that form the bedrock of cross-border financial investigations. This exploration is not just about understanding the law; it's about appreciating its rationale and its pivotal role in facilitating justice while respecting the nuances of international relations.

In an era where data is as valuable as currency, safeguarding privacy while pursuing justice presents a unique conundrum. This chapter dives deep into the realm of data privacy, illuminating the principles that govern the collection, analysis, and sharing of information in financial investigations. We navigate through legislation such as the General Data Protection Regulation (GDPR) and others, understanding their implications for investigators and the individuals whose data is pivotal to inquiries.

Collaboration is the linchpin in dismantling transnational financial crimes. This section elucidates the mechanisms of international cooperation, from Interpol's networks to bilateral agreements, and how these facilitate the seamless flow of crucial investigative information across borders. It's a testament to how shared goals and mutual understanding can forge alliances against a common adversary.

While law provides the framework, ethics offer the moral grounding essential for investigators. This chapter emphasizes the ethical considerations that must guide every action, decision, and interaction in the realm of financial investigations, ensuring that the pursuit of justice is never compromised by the means employed to achieve it.

Real-world case studies provide the narrative to the theories and principles discussed, offering insights into the application of legal and cooperative strategies in high-stakes investigations. These stories highlight successes, reveal challenges, and underscore the indispensable role of legal and ethical adherence in the realm of international financial investigations.

As we gaze into the future, this chapter also contemplates the evolving legal landscapes and the implications for financial investigators. In a world where financial crimes increasingly leverage technology, staying abreast of legal developments and international cooperation frameworks is paramount.

Chapter 6 is more than just a guide; it's a manifesto for conducting financial investigations with legal integrity and ethical clarity. It prepares investigators to not only navigate but to thrive in the intricate legal terrain of international financial forensics, ensuring that their endeavors are as lawful as they are tenacious.

6.1 Understanding Data Privacy Laws

Data privacy laws and regulations play a crucial role in digital financial investigations. Investigators must ensure that their collection, analysis, and use of personal data comply with all applicable laws to protect the privacy of individuals and maintain the integrity of the investigation.

Some of the key data privacy laws and regulations that investigators need to be aware of include:

General Data Protection Regulation (GDPR): The GDPR is a comprehensive data privacy law that applies to the processing of personal data of individuals within the European Union. It grants individuals various rights regarding their personal data, including the right to access, rectify, and erase their data.

California Consumer Privacy Act (CCPA): The CCPA is a data privacy law that applies to the processing of personal data of California residents. It grants consumers similar rights to those provided by the GDPR.

Other national and regional data privacy laws: Many countries and regions have their own data privacy laws and regulations that investigators need to be aware of when conducting investigations in those jurisdictions.

These laws typically require investigators to:

Obtain consent: In many cases, investigators need to obtain consent from individuals before collecting or processing their personal data.

Provide notice: Individuals need to be informed about how their data is being collected, used, and stored.

Ensure data security: Investigators must take appropriate measures to protect personal data from unauthorized access, use, or disclosure.

Grant individuals access to their data: Individuals have the right to access their personal data and request corrections or erasure.

For example, if investigators need to access the financial records of a suspect who is a resident of the European Union, they must comply with the GDPR. This may involve obtaining consent from the suspect, providing notice about how the data will be used, and ensuring that the data is securely stored and protected.

What are some of the challenges associated with complying with data privacy laws in financial investigations?

Complying with data privacy laws can be challenging for financial investigators, as these laws can be complex and vary across jurisdictions. Investigators need to be familiar with the specific requirements of the applicable laws and ensure that their investigative methods comply with these requirements. Additionally, balancing the need for effective investigations with the protection of individual privacy can be a delicate task.

By understanding data privacy laws and implementing appropriate safeguards, investigators can conduct their investigations in a lawful and ethical manner while protecting the privacy of individuals.

6.2 Complying with Financial Regulations

Financial investigations often involve navigating a complex web of financial regulations designed to prevent and detect financial crimes. Investigators need to be familiar with these regulations and ensure that their actions comply with all applicable requirements.

Some of the key financial regulations that investigators need to be aware of include:

Anti-Money Laundering (AML) and Know Your Customer (KYC) regulations: These regulations require financial institutions to implement measures to prevent money laundering and terrorist financing. This includes verifying the identities of their customers, monitoring transactions for suspicious activity, and reporting suspicious transactions to authorities.

Securities regulations: These regulations govern the trading of securities and aim to protect investors from fraud and other illegal activities. Investigators need to be aware of these regulations when investigating insider trading, market manipulation, and other securities-related crimes.

Tax regulations: Tax laws and regulations can be relevant in financial investigations, especially when investigating tax evasion or fraud. Investigators may need to collaborate with tax authorities to obtain information and build cases.

Investigators may also need to comply with international financial regulations, such as the Financial Action Task Force (FATF) recommendations, when conducting cross-border investigations. This may involve coordinating with foreign authorities and navigating different legal and regulatory frameworks.

For example, investigators investigating a suspected money laundering scheme may need to work with financial institutions to obtain KYC/AML data and transaction records. They may also need to report suspicious transactions to the relevant authorities.

What are some of the challenges associated with complying with financial regulations in cross-border investigations?

Complying with financial regulations in cross-border investigations can be challenging due to the different legal and regulatory frameworks across jurisdictions. Investigators may need to navigate complex legal processes to obtain information from foreign financial institutions or authorities. Additionally, differences in data privacy laws and regulations can further complicate cross-border investigations.

By understanding the relevant financial regulations and collaborating with international partners, investigators can ensure that their cross-border investigations are conducted in a lawful and effective manner.

6.3 Obtaining Legal Assistance and Cooperation

Financial investigations often require obtaining legal assistance and cooperation from various parties, including:

Legal counsel: Investigators should seek guidance from legal counsel to ensure that their investigative methods comply with all applicable laws and regulations. Legal counsel can also assist with obtaining warrants, subpoenas, and other legal instruments needed to access information and evidence.

Law enforcement agencies: Investigators may need to collaborate with law enforcement agencies to obtain assistance with search warrants, arrests, and other law enforcement actions.

Regulatory authorities: Depending on the nature of the investigation, investigators may need to work with regulatory authorities, such as financial regulators or tax authorities, to obtain information and build a case.

Foreign authorities: Cross-border financial investigations often require cooperation with foreign authorities to obtain evidence and apprehend suspects. This may involve navigating complex legal processes and international treaties.

Effective collaboration and communication are crucial for obtaining legal assistance and cooperation. Investigators need to clearly communicate their needs and objectives to other parties and build strong working relationships to ensure successful outcomes.

For example, investigators investigating a cross-border money laundering scheme might need to obtain legal assistance from foreign authorities to access bank records and interview witnesses in another country. This would require navigating international legal processes and establishing cooperation with foreign counterparts.

What are some of the challenges associated with obtaining legal assistance and cooperation in cross-border financial investigations?

Obtaining legal assistance and cooperation in cross-border financial investigations can be challenging due to differences in legal systems, data privacy laws, and investigative procedures. Investigators may need to overcome language barriers, navigate complex legal processes, and build trust with foreign authorities.

By understanding the legal and regulatory frameworks in different jurisdictions and establishing strong working relationships with foreign counterparts, investigators can facilitate cooperation and obtain the assistance they need to conduct effective cross-border investigations.

6.4 Handling Evidence and Ensuring Admissibility

The way evidence is collected, preserved, and presented can significantly impact its admissibility in court. In digital financial investigations, it is crucial to handle digital evidence with care to ensure its integrity and admissibility.

Best practices for handling digital evidence include:

Chain of custody: Maintain a clear and documented chain of custody for all evidence, including digital evidence. This involves documenting who collected the evidence, when it was collected, and how it was stored and transferred.

Preservation: Digital evidence can be easily altered or destroyed. Investigators must take steps to preserve the evidence in its original form, such as creating forensic copies and using write-blocking tools.

Authentication: Investigators need to be able to authenticate digital evidence to demonstrate that it is genuine and has not been tampered with. This may involve using hashing algorithms or other technical methods.

Documentation: All actions taken with regard to the evidence should be carefully documented, including the collection, preservation, and analysis processes.

Failure to follow these best practices can result in the exclusion of evidence from court proceedings, which can significantly weaken the case against the accused.

For example, investigators might use specialized forensic tools to collect digital evidence from a suspect's computer. They would then need to document the collection process, create forensic copies of the evidence, and store the evidence securely to maintain its integrity.

What are some of the challenges associated with handling and ensuring the admissibility of digital evidence?

Digital evidence can be easily altered or destroyed, making it crucial to follow strict chain of custody procedures and preservation techniques. Additionally, the authentication of digital evidence can be complex, and investigators need to be familiar with the latest forensic tools and techniques to ensure that the evidence is admissible in court.

By following best practices and collaborating with forensic experts, investigators can ensure that digital evidence is collected, preserved, and presented in a way that meets legal standards and strengthens the case against financial criminals.

6.5 Balancing Investigative Needs with Privacy Rights

Financial investigations often involve collecting and analyzing personal data, which can raise privacy concerns. Investigators must balance the need for effective investigations with the protection of individual privacy rights.

Some key considerations for balancing investigative needs with privacy rights include:

Legality: Investigators must ensure that their actions comply with all applicable data privacy laws and regulations. This includes obtaining necessary consents, providing notice to individuals, and implementing appropriate data security measures.

Proportionality: The collection and use of personal data should be proportionate to the legitimate aims of the investigation. Investigators should only collect and analyze data that is relevant and necessary for the investigation.

Transparency: Investigators should be transparent about their data collection and analysis practices and provide individuals with access to their personal data upon request.

Data minimization: Investigators should only collect and store the minimum amount of personal data necessary for the investigation.

Data security: Investigators must implement appropriate data security measures to protect personal data from unauthorized access, use, or disclosure.

For example, investigators might need to access the financial records of individuals during an investigation. They should only access the records that are relevant to the investigation, ensure that the data is securely stored, and provide individuals with access to their data upon request.

What are some of the challenges associated with balancing investigative needs with privacy rights in the digital age?

The digital age has created new challenges for balancing investigative needs with privacy rights. The vast amount of personal data available online and the increasing use of surveillance technologies can make it difficult to protect individual privacy while conducting effective investigations.

By adhering to data privacy laws, adopting ethical investigative practices, and utilizing data minimization and security measures, investigators can strike a balance between investigative needs and the protection of individual privacy rights.

Chapter 7: Building a Case: Evidence Collection, Preservation, and Presentation

"Facts are stubborn things; and whatever may be our wishes, our inclinations, or the dictates of our passions, they cannot alter the state of facts and evidence." - John Adams

Embark on a journey through Chapter 7, where the mosaic of financial investigations comes into sharp focus, converging at the pivotal point of evidence collection, preservation, and presentation. This chapter is a deep dive into the bedrock of any financial investigation—the meticulous and methodical approach to handling evidence that can make or break a case. It's here that the intricate dance of assembling, safeguarding, and articulating evidence unfolds, guiding investigators through the labyrinthine process that underpins the quest for truth and accountability in financial crimes.

Evidence is the cornerstone upon which the edifice of justice is built. In this chapter, we dissect the multifaceted process of evidence collection, where precision meets diligence. We explore the strategies and best practices for gathering evidence, emphasizing the importance of a methodical approach that ensures no stone is left unturned in the pursuit of irrefutable proof.

Preservation is the guardian of evidence's soul. It's not merely about holding onto evidence but about maintaining its integrity, ensuring that its voice remains untarnished when it speaks in the halls of justice. We delve into the protocols and precautions that protect evidence from contamination or tampering, ensuring its pristine condition and the continuity of its narrative.

The presentation of evidence is where the symphony of facts and findings resonates, telling the story that needs to be heard. This chapter guides investigators on how to transform a collection of individual pieces of evidence into a coherent and compelling narrative, employing techniques that enhance clarity and impact, ensuring that the evidence not only speaks but resonates.

In the realm of financial investigations, the legal framework is both a map and a compass. We navigate the legal nuances of handling evidence, from the chain of custody to the admissibility in court, ensuring that investigators are equipped with the knowledge to maneuver through the legal labyrinth with confidence and acumen.

Through real-world case studies, this chapter illuminates the principles of evidence handling in action, showcasing how theoretical knowledge is applied in practical scenarios. These narratives offer a window into the challenges and triumphs of investigators, providing insights and lessons that enrich understanding and inspire excellence.

As we peer into the future, we consider the evolving landscape of evidence in financial investigations, contemplating the impact of emerging technologies and shifting legal paradigms. This chapter prepares investigators for the future, encouraging adaptability and a forward-looking approach to evidence handling.

In Chapter 7, investigators are equipped with the tools, knowledge, and insights necessary to master the art and science of evidence in financial investigations. It's a chapter that transforms evidence from a mere collection of data and artifacts into the powerful testament that underpins the quest for justice in the complex world of financial crime.

7.1 Developing an Evidence Collection Plan

A well-defined evidence collection plan is crucial for ensuring that all relevant evidence is collected efficiently and effectively while maintaining its integrity and admissibility.

Key steps in developing an evidence collection plan include:

Identifying the types of evidence: Investigators need to identify the specific types of evidence that are relevant to the case. This may include financial records, emails, digital files, physical documents, and witness statements.

Prioritizing collection efforts: Not all evidence is equally important. Investigators should prioritize the collection of the most critical and time-sensitive evidence first.

Determining collection methods: Different types of evidence require different collection methods. Investigators need to determine the appropriate methods and tools for collecting each type of evidence while ensuring its integrity.

Assigning responsibilities: Clear roles and responsibilities should be assigned to team members involved in evidence collection.

Documenting the process: All steps of the evidence collection process should be carefully documented to maintain chain of custody and ensure admissibility.

The evidence collection plan should be flexible and adaptable to accommodate new information and developments that may arise during the investigation.

For example, in a case involving suspected embezzlement, the evidence collection plan might prioritize the collection of financial records, bank statements, and internal emails. Investigators would need to determine the appropriate methods for collecting this evidence, such as obtaining warrants or subpoenas, and assign responsibilities to team members for collecting and preserving the evidence.

What are some of the challenges associated with developing an evidence collection plan in digital financial investigations?

Crafting an evidence collection plan in the realm of digital financial investigations presents a set of nuanced challenges, each demanding a meticulous approach and a profound understanding of the digital world. As financial crimes evolve with technology, investigators are tasked with developing strategies that are not only effective but also adaptable to the changing digital landscape.

Handling the Volume and Diversity of Digital Evidence

One of the primary hurdles in developing an evidence collection plan is the sheer volume of digital evidence. The proliferation of digital devices and online platforms has led to an exponential increase in data that can be relevant to financial investigations. This abundance of data requires investigators to be discerning in identifying and collecting pertinent evidence, necessitating a plan that is both comprehensive and targeted.

Moreover, the diversity of digital evidence adds layers of complexity to the planning process. Financial investigators must contend with various data formats, storage mediums, and technologies. From traditional computer systems to cloud storage and mobile devices, each potential source of evidence demands specific collection methods and tools, making the development of a one-size-fits-all plan virtually impossible.

Staying Abreast of Forensic Tools and Techniques

The landscape of digital forensics is continually evolving, with new tools and techniques emerging to address the latest technologies and encryption methods. An effective evidence collection plan must incorporate the most current and robust forensic tools available. However, keeping up with these advancements requires ongoing training and awareness, posing a challenge for investigators who must balance their casework with professional development.

Ensuring the Integrity and Admissibility of Digital Evidence

The dynamic nature of digital evidence poses significant challenges in maintaining its integrity and admissibility in a legal context. Digital data can be easily altered, deleted, or corrupted, necessitating stringent protocols for its collection, storage, and analysis. The evidence collection plan must detail these protocols, ensuring that every piece of collected evidence can withstand legal scrutiny.

Chain of custody is a critical component of this process. Each step, from the initial collection to the final presentation in court, must be meticulously documented and secure. Any lapse in this chain can compromise the evidence, potentially undermining the investigation and subsequent legal proceedings.

Addressing Legal and Ethical Considerations

Legal and ethical considerations are paramount in developing an evidence collection plan. Digital investigations often tread a fine line between thorough investigation and respect for privacy rights. Investigators must navigate various jurisdictions' laws, which can vary significantly, particularly when dealing with international cases or cloud-based data stored in different countries.

Moreover, the ethical implications of surveillance, data collection, and privacy must be considered. Plans must be developed with a clear understanding of what is legally permissible and ethically justifiable, balancing the pursuit of justice with respect for individual rights.

Managing Resources and Time Constraints

Resource allocation is another critical aspect of developing an evidence collection plan. Digital investigations can be resource-intensive, requiring specialized tools, expertise, and significant time investment. Efficient resource management is crucial, ensuring that the investigative team has the necessary tools and expertise without straining the department's overall resources.

Time is also a critical factor, especially given the volatile nature of digital evidence. Data can be quickly changed or deleted, and cloud-based information can be ephemeral. Therefore, the evidence collection plan must prioritize swift action, ensuring that vital evidence is secured before it's altered or lost.

In conclusion, developing an evidence collection plan in digital financial investigations is a multifaceted challenge that requires a deep understanding of digital technologies, forensic methodologies, legal frameworks, and ethical considerations. By addressing these challenges with meticulous planning, continuous learning, and strategic resource management, investigators can effectively gather the evidence needed to unravel complex financial crimes in the digital age.

7.2 Ensuring Proper Chain of Custody

Chain of custody refers to the documented and verifiable history of the evidence from the time it is collected until it is presented in court. Maintaining proper chain of custody is crucial for ensuring the integrity of the evidence and its admissibility in legal proceedings.

Best practices for ensuring proper chain of custody include:

Documentation: Every step of the evidence handling process should be carefully documented, including who collected the evidence, when it was collected, who it was transferred to, and the storage conditions.

Unique identifiers: Each piece of evidence should be assigned a unique identifier to track its movement and prevent confusion.

Secure storage: Evidence should be stored in a secure location with limited access to prevent tampering or contamination.

Transfer procedures: Strict procedures should be followed when transferring evidence from one person or location to another. This includes documenting the transfer and ensuring that the evidence is properly packaged and sealed.

Maintaining chain of custody can be particularly challenging in digital financial investigations due to the dynamic nature of digital evidence. Investigators need to take special precautions to prevent alteration or contamination of digital evidence.

For example, when collecting digital evidence from a suspect's computer, investigators should use write-blocking tools to prevent any changes to the data. They should also create forensic copies of the evidence and store the original evidence in a secure location.

What are some of the challenges associated with maintaining chain of custody in digital financial investigations?

In digital financial investigations, maintaining an unbroken chain of custody for digital evidence is paramount, yet fraught with challenges. This critical process, which documents the collection, transfer, handling, and storage of evidence, is essential for ensuring its integrity and admissibility in legal proceedings. The digital nature of the evidence, however, introduces specific obstacles that investigators must adeptly navigate.

Vulnerability to Alteration and Destruction

Digital evidence, inherently malleable, can be easily modified, copied, or deleted without leaving apparent physical traces. This characteristic poses a significant challenge, as even minor, inadvertent changes can undermine the evidence's integrity. Ensuring that digital data remains unaltered from the point of collection to its presentation in court requires meticulous handling and advanced technical measures.

Complexity of Digital Environments

The environments where digital evidence resides are varied and complex, ranging from individual devices to expansive networks and cloud services. Each environment demands specific protocols for evidence extraction to maintain the chain of custody. For instance, extracting data from a cloud-based service differs vastly from retrieving it from a physical hard drive, with each process requiring distinct tools and expertise.

Implementing Strict Handling Procedures

To counter the risk of contamination or tampering, strict procedures must be established for every phase of handling digital evidence. This includes creating forensic copies of data (ensuring original data remains untouched), using write blockers when accessing storage devices, and employing cryptographic hashes to verify data integrity. Each step must be precisely documented, detailing who accessed the evidence, when, why, and what actions were taken.

Documentation and Log Keeping

Effective documentation is the backbone of a robust chain of custody. Every interaction with the evidence must be logged in detail, creating a transparent trail that can be followed and verified by others, including the court. This documentation must be both comprehensive and comprehensible, capable of withstanding scrutiny from legal experts, opposing counsel, and the judiciary.

Training and Competency of Investigators

Maintaining the chain of custody in a digital realm requires a specific skill set. Investigators must not only be proficient in the technical aspects of handling digital evidence but also understand the legal implications of their actions. Continuous training is essential, as both technology and legal standards evolve, demanding ongoing learning and adaptation from the investigators.

Storage and Access Controls

The storage of digital evidence is as crucial as its collection. Secure, controlled environments are necessary to protect evidence from unauthorized access or environmental hazards (e.g., magnetic fields, moisture, or physical shocks). Moreover, access to this evidence must be strictly controlled and monitored, with entry logged and audited to ensure that only authorized personnel can interact with the evidence.

Legal and Jurisdictional Challenges

The global nature of digital data introduces legal complexities, particularly when evidence spans multiple jurisdictions with differing legal standards and requirements for evidence handling. Investigators must navigate these legal landscapes, ensuring that chain of custody protocols meet the requisite standards across all relevant jurisdictions.

In essence, while the digitalization of financial transactions and communications presents new avenues for investigating financial crimes, it also demands rigorous standards for evidence handling. By addressing the unique challenges of maintaining the chain of custody in digital contexts, investigators can safeguard the integrity of their evidence, supporting the pursuit of justice in an increasingly digital world.

7.3 Preserving Digital Evidence

Digital evidence is often fragile and dynamic, making its preservation a critical aspect of financial investigations. Investigators must take appropriate steps to ensure that digital evidence is preserved in its original form and protected from alteration or destruction.

Some common methods for preserving digital evidence include:

Creating forensic copies: Forensic copies are exact duplicates of the original digital evidence. These copies are created using specialized tools and techniques to ensure that the original evidence remains unaltered.

Write-blocking: Write-blocking tools prevent any changes from being made to the original digital evidence. This ensures that the evidence remains in its original state and can be authenticated later.

Hashing: Hashing algorithms can be used to create unique digital fingerprints of the evidence. These fingerprints can be used to verify that the evidence has not been altered since it was collected.

Secure storage: Digital evidence should be stored in a secure location with limited access to prevent unauthorized modification or deletion. This may involve using encrypted storage devices and secure cloud storage solutions.

It is important to note that different types of digital evidence may require different preservation methods. Investigators should consult with forensic experts to determine the most appropriate preservation techniques for each type of evidence.

For example, investigators might create forensic copies of digital files found on a suspect's computer and store the original files in a secure, write-blocked storage device. This ensures that the evidence is preserved in its original form and can be authenticated later.

What are some of the challenges associated with preserving digital evidence in financial investigations?

Preserving digital evidence can be challenging due to its dynamic nature and the ease with which it can be altered or destroyed. Investigators need to be familiar with specialized tools and techniques for preserving digital evidence and implement strict procedures to ensure its integrity. Additionally, the increasing use of encryption and cloud storage can present challenges for accessing and preserving digital evidence.

By following best practices and collaborating with forensic experts, investigators can ensure that digital evidence is properly preserved and admissible in court.

7.4 Analyzing and Interpreting Evidence

Once evidence has been collected and preserved, investigators need to analyze and interpret it to draw meaningful conclusions and build a strong case. This involves:

Organizing and reviewing the evidence: Investigators need to organize the evidence in a way that allows for efficient review and analysis. This may involve creating timelines, spreadsheets, and other visual aids.

Identifying patterns and connections: Investigators should look for patterns and connections in the evidence that may indicate fraudulent activity or link suspects to the crime.

Utilizing data analysis tools: Data analysis tools can help investigators identify anomalies, trends, and hidden connections in large datasets.

Collaborating with experts: Investigators may need to collaborate with financial experts, forensic specialists, and other experts to interpret complex evidence and draw accurate conclusions.

It is important to document the analysis process and the conclusions drawn from the evidence. This documentation will be crucial for presenting the evidence in court and demonstrating the rationale behind the investigators' conclusions.

For example, investigators might analyze financial records and transaction data to identify patterns of suspicious activity. They might also use data analysis tools to identify anomalies and connections that suggest fraudulent intent.

What are some of the challenges associated with analyzing and interpreting evidence in digital financial investigations?

Analyzing and interpreting evidence in digital financial investigations can be challenging due to the volume and complexity of the data. Investigators need to be familiar with specialized tools and techniques for data analysis and interpretation. Additionally, the dynamic nature of digital evidence and the increasing use of encryption and anonymizing technologies can present challenges for investigators.

By collaborating with experts, utilizing appropriate tools and techniques, and documenting their analysis process, investigators can effectively analyze and interpret evidence to build strong cases against financial criminals.

7.5 Presenting Evidence Effectively

Presenting evidence effectively is crucial for convincing a judge, jury, or other decision-makers of the guilt of the accused. In digital financial investigations, presenting evidence can be particularly challenging due to the complexity of the data and the need to explain technical concepts to a non-technical audience.

Best practices for presenting evidence effectively include:

Clarity and conciseness: Present the evidence in a clear and concise manner, avoiding technical jargon and complex explanations whenever possible.

Visual aids: Utilize visual aids, such as charts, graphs, and timelines, to present complex data in a way that is easy to understand.

Storytelling: Frame the evidence in a compelling narrative that explains the sequence of events and the motivations of the accused.

Credibility and objectivity: Present the evidence in a credible and objective manner, avoiding speculation and personal opinions.

Tailoring the presentation: Tailor the presentation of evidence to the specific audience, whether it be law enforcement, regulators, or a court of law.

By following these best practices, investigators can effectively communicate the findings of their investigation and increase the likelihood of a successful outcome.

For example, investigators might use a timeline to present the sequence of events in a financial fraud case. They might also use charts and graphs to illustrate the flow of funds and highlight suspicious transactions.

What are some of the challenges associated with presenting digital evidence effectively?

Presenting digital evidence in legal settings introduces unique challenges that investigators must adeptly navigate to ensure their findings are understood and impactful. The essence of these challenges lies in translating complex digital data into a format that's accessible and persuasive to a non-technical audience, typically comprised of judges, jurors, and legal professionals.

Simplifying Complex Information

Digital evidence often encompasses intricate technical details that can be perplexing to those without a background in digital forensics. Investigators must distill this complexity into simpler concepts without compromising the evidence's integrity. This distillation process is crucial for ensuring that the audience grasps the relevance and significance of the evidence.

Creating Clear and Compelling Narratives

Effective communication of digital evidence requires more than just simplification; it necessitates the creation of a coherent narrative. Investigators must weave the digital data into a storyline that elucidates the sequence of events, the actions of the involved parties, and the evidence's implications. This storytelling approach can help make the digital evidence more relatable and memorable for the audience.

Utilizing Visual Aids

Visual aids can be instrumental in clarifying and emphasizing key points of digital evidence. Diagrams, charts, timelines, and other graphical representations can help demystify complex data, making it more accessible. These visuals need to be well-designed, focusing on clarity and relevance to support the narrative effectively.

Engaging and Persuasive Delivery

The delivery of the presentation is as vital as its content. Investigators must be articulate and engaging, capable of maintaining the audience's attention and interest. This requires a balance of professionalism and approachability, ensuring that the presentation is not only informative but also persuasive.

Tailoring Presentations to the Audience

Understanding the audience is essential for effective presentation. Investigators should tailor their language, examples, and emphasis based on the audience's level of technical expertise and their role in the legal process. This tailored approach can enhance comprehension and engagement, making the digital evidence more impactful.

Addressing Potential Skepticism

Given the intangible nature of digital data, investigators might encounter skepticism regarding the evidence's reliability and relevance. Anticipating and addressing these concerns within the presentation can help reinforce the evidence's credibility. This might involve explaining the methods used to preserve the data's integrity and the processes followed to analyze it.

Legal and Procedural Adherence

Presenting digital evidence also involves navigating legal protocols and evidentiary standards. Investigators must ensure that their presentation aligns with the legal requirements, addressing admissibility issues, and respecting the procedural norms of the legal setting.

Continuous Learning and Adaptation

Finally, given the rapid evolution of technology, investigators must continually update their knowledge and adapt their presentation strategies. Staying informed about the latest digital trends, tools, and presentation techniques can help investigators remain effective and persuasive in their evidence presentation.

In summary, the effective presentation of digital evidence requires a multifaceted approach, combining technical expertise with communication skills and legal acumen. By addressing these challenges, investigators can enhance the clarity, relevance, and persuasive power of digital evidence, facilitating a clearer understanding and aiding the pursuit of justice in the digital realm.

Chapter 8: The Future of Financial Investigations: Emerging Technologies and Trends

"The best way to predict the future is to create it." - Abraham Lincoln

Embark on a visionary journey through Chapter 8, where we step beyond the present and peer into the dynamic future of financial investigations. As the digital age accelerates, bringing forth new technologies and methodologies, the landscape of financial crime and its investigation is in constant evolution. This chapter is a forward-looking exploration, offering a glimpse into the emerging trends, technologies, and challenges that will shape the future of financial investigations.

In this era of rapid technological advancement, emerging tools and methodologies are set to redefine the arsenal of financial investigators. From the integration of artificial intelligence and machine learning to the utilization of blockchain technology, this chapter delves into how these innovations are transforming the field, offering new avenues for detection, analysis, and resolution of financial crimes.

Just as investigative techniques evolve, so too do the methods of those engaged in financial malfeasance. We explore the anticipated shifts in the landscape of financial crime, considering how globalization, digital currency, and cyber advancements are creating new challenges and opportunities for those on both sides of the law.

The future of financial investigations demands adaptability and foresight. This chapter examines how investigators can stay ahead of the curve, adapting their strategies to meet the complexities of future financial crimes. We discuss the importance of continuous learning, cross-disciplinary collaboration, and the integration of new tools into the investigative process.

As the boundaries of financial investigations expand, so too do the ethical considerations. This chapter provides a thoughtful exploration of the ethical implications of new investigative technologies and methodologies, emphasizing the importance of maintaining a balance between innovative investigation techniques and the protection of individual rights and privacy.

Through speculative case studies, this chapter provides a practical perspective on how future trends and technologies might play out in real-world scenarios. These narratives serve as a bridge between theoretical exploration and practical application, offering a tangible sense of how the future of financial investigations could unfold.

In conclusion, Chapter 8 is not merely a forecast but a preparation for the uncharted journey ahead. It equips financial investigators with the insights, knowledge, and foresight needed to navigate the evolving terrain of financial crime and its investigation. As we stand on the brink of future advancements, this chapter serves as a beacon, guiding investigators toward a proactive, informed, and strategic approach to the challenges and opportunities that lie ahead.

In this chapter, we embrace the future, not as a distant horizon but as an imminent reality, preparing financial investigators to adapt, innovate, and thrive in the dynamic landscape of financial investigations that awaits.

8.1 The Rise of Artificial Intelligence and Machine Learning

Artificial intelligence (AI) and machine learning (ML) are rapidly transforming various industries, including the field of financial investigations. These technologies have the potential to significantly enhance the effectiveness and efficiency of investigations by automating tasks, analyzing vast amounts of data, and identifying complex patterns and connections.

Some of the ways AI and ML can be used in financial investigations include:

Fraud detection: AI and ML algorithms can be trained to identify patterns and anomalies in financial data that may indicate fraudulent activity. This can help investigators detect fraud earlier and prevent financial losses.

Transaction monitoring: AI and ML can be used to monitor financial transactions in real-time and flag suspicious activities for further investigation.

Network analysis: AI and ML can be used to analyze complex financial networks and identify key players, influencers, and potential co-conspirators.

Predictive analytics: AI and ML can be used to predict future fraudulent activity based on historical data and patterns. This can help investigators take proactive measures to prevent financial crimes.

While AI and ML offer significant potential for financial investigations, it is important to note that these technologies also present challenges:

Bias: AI and ML algorithms can be biased based on the data they are trained on. Investigators need to be aware of these biases and take steps to mitigate them.

Transparency: The decision-making processes of AI and ML algorithms can be complex and opaque. Investigators need to be able to explain and justify the findings of AI and ML tools.

Ethical considerations: The use of AI and ML in investigations raises ethical concerns, such as the potential for privacy violations and discrimination. Investigators need to use these technologies responsibly and ethically.

For example, investigators might use an AI-powered fraud detection system to analyze credit card transactions and identify potential fraudulent activity. The system could be trained to identify patterns and anomalies that are associated with fraud, such as transactions from unusual locations or for unusually large amounts.

What are some of the ethical considerations associated with using AI and ML in financial investigations?

The use of AI and ML in financial investigations raises ethical concerns, such as the potential for privacy violations and discrimination. Investigators need to ensure that these technologies are used responsibly and ethically, and that they do not disproportionately target certain individuals or groups. Additionally, investigators need to be transparent about their use of AI and ML and ensure that the decision-making processes of these tools are fair and unbiased.

By using AI and ML responsibly and ethically, investigators can leverage the power of these technologies to enhance the effectiveness and efficiency of financial investigations while protecting the rights and privacy of individuals.

8.2 Blockchain Technology and its Impact

Blockchain technology is transforming the financial landscape, and its impact is also being felt in the field of financial investigations. Blockchain is a distributed ledger technology that allows for secure, transparent, and immutable record-keeping. This has significant implications for tracing financial transactions and investigating financial crimes.

Some of the ways blockchain technology is impacting financial investigations include:

Enhanced transparency: Blockchain transactions are publicly viewable and immutable, providing investigators with a transparent and reliable record of financial activities.

Improved traceability: Blockchain forensics tools can be used to trace cryptocurrency transactions and identify the parties involved, even if they are using pseudonymous wallets.

Reduced fraud: The immutability of blockchain records makes it more difficult for criminals to manipulate financial data or commit fraud.

New investigative tools: Blockchain forensics tools and techniques are constantly evolving, providing investigators with new capabilities to trace transactions and uncover illicit activities.

However, blockchain technology also presents challenges for investigators:

Anonymity: While blockchain transactions are publicly viewable, the identities of the individuals behind the wallets are often obscured. This can make it difficult to identify suspects and link them to real-world identities.

Transaction mixing: Criminals can use mixing services to obscure the flow of funds, making it more difficult to trace transactions.

Cross-border transactions: Cryptocurrency transactions can easily cross borders, which can complicate investigations and require cooperation with foreign authorities.

For example, investigators might use blockchain forensics to trace the flow of funds in a ransomware attack. By analyzing the blockchain data, investigators can identify the wallet address used by the attacker to receive the ransom payment. This information can then be used to try to identify the attacker and recover the stolen funds.

What are some of the emerging trends in blockchain technology that are relevant to financial investigations?

Blockchain technology is constantly evolving, and new applications are being developed all the time. Some emerging trends that are relevant to financial investigations include:

Central bank digital currencies (CBDCs): Central banks around the world are exploring the development of CBDCs, which could provide greater transparency and traceability for financial transactions.

Decentralized finance (DeFi): DeFi applications are providing new ways to conduct financial transactions without the need for traditional intermediaries. This presents new challenges and opportunities for financial investigators.

Non-fungible tokens (NFTs): NFTs are being used to represent ownership of digital assets. Investigators need to be aware of how NFTs can be used in financial crimes, such as money laundering and fraud.

By staying informed about the latest developments in blockchain technology, investigators can adapt their strategies and techniques to effectively combat financial crime in the digital age.

8.3 The Growing Importance of Cybersecurity

As financial crimes increasingly move online, cybersecurity plays a crucial role in preventing, detecting, and investigating these crimes. Financial institutions and other organizations need to implement robust cybersecurity measures to protect their systems and data from cyberattacks.

Some key aspects of cybersecurity relevant to financial investigations include:

Network security: Protecting computer networks from unauthorized access, use, or disclosure. This includes implementing firewalls, intrusion detection systems, and other security measures.

Data security: Protecting sensitive financial data from unauthorized access, use, or disclosure. This includes implementing encryption, access controls, and data loss prevention measures.

Incident response: Having plans and procedures in place to respond to cyberattacks effectively. This includes identifying and containing the attack, recovering lost data, and preventing future attacks.

Cybersecurity awareness training: Educating employees and stakeholders about cybersecurity risks and best practices to prevent cyberattacks.

Cybersecurity professionals play a vital role in financial investigations by:

Identifying and preserving digital evidence: *Cybersecurity professionals can help investigators identify and preserve digital evidence from cyberattacks, such as malware, phishing emails, and network logs.*

Real-World Example: The DNC Hack and the 2016 US Election Interference

The 2016 hack of the Democratic National Committee (DNC) servers serves as a prime example of cybersecurity professionals identifying and preserving digital evidence in a high-profile cyberattack with significant real-world consequences.

What Happened:

2016: Hackers, later attributed to Russian intelligence agencies, infiltrated the DNC's computer network and stole sensitive data, including emails and internal documents.

Leaked Information: The stolen data was subsequently leaked online and published through platforms like WikiLeaks, causing significant political controversy during the 2016 US presidential election.

Role of Cybersecurity Professionals:

Incident Response: Cybersecurity firms like CrowdStrike were called in to investigate the breach, identify the attackers, and assess the extent of the damage.

Evidence Collection and Preservation: Experts analyzed network logs, malware samples, and other digital artifacts to trace the attackers' activities and gather evidence of their methods and origins.

Attribution: Through meticulous analysis of the evidence, cybersecurity professionals were able to link the attack to specific hacking groups with ties to the Russian government.

Evidence and its Impact:

Technical Indicators: Experts identified specific malware tools and techniques used in the attack that were known to be associated with Russian hacking groups.

Network Traffic Analysis: Tracing the source of the attacks through network logs and IP addresses further corroborated the link to Russia.

Political and Legal Consequences: The evidence gathered by cybersecurity professionals played a crucial role in investigations by US intelligence agencies and the Special Counsel investigation into Russian interference in the election.

Lessons Learned:

The DNC hack underscored the vulnerability of political organizations and campaigns to cyberattacks and the importance of robust cybersecurity measures. It also highlighted the critical role of cybersecurity professionals in identifying, preserving, and analyzing digital evidence to attribute cyberattacks and hold perpetrators accountable.

Additional Points:

The incident sparked a broader discussion about election security and the potential for foreign interference in democratic processes.

The case demonstrated the challenges of attributing cyberattacks to specific actors, particularly when nation-states are involved.

Cybersecurity professionals continue to develop and refine techniques for evidence collection and analysis to combat increasingly sophisticated cyber threats.

Analyzing cyberattacks: *Cybersecurity professionals can analyze cyberattacks to determine the methods used by the attackers, the extent of the damage, and the potential source of the attack.*

Real-World Example: The SolarWinds Supply Chain Attack

The SolarWinds supply chain attack, discovered in late 2020, offers a complex and impactful example of cybersecurity professionals analyzing a large-scale cyberattack to understand the methods, damage, and origins.

What Happened:

Compromised Software: Hackers, believed to be linked to the Russian government, infiltrated the systems of SolarWinds, a company that provides IT management software to numerous government agencies and private companies.

Supply Chain Attack: The attackers injected malicious code into SolarWinds' Orion software updates, which were then distributed to thousands of the company's customers.

Extensive Reach: The attack impacted numerous organizations, including major US government agencies like the Department of Homeland Security, the Treasury Department, and the Department of Commerce.

Analysis by Cybersecurity Professionals:

Malware Analysis: Experts analyzed the malicious code (dubbed Sunburst) to understand its functionalities and how it compromised systems. They discovered that the malware allowed attackers to establish backdoors, steal data, and move laterally within compromised networks.

Network Forensics: Analyzing network logs and traffic patterns helped investigators trace the attackers' activities and identify the extent of the compromise.

Attribution: Based on the tools, techniques, and infrastructure used in the attack, cybersecurity professionals and intelligence agencies attributed the attack to a group known as APT29 or Cozy Bear, linked to the Russian Foreign Intelligence Service (SVR).

Extent of Damage and Impact:

Data Breaches: The attackers were able to steal sensitive data from numerous organizations, including government agencies.

Espionage: The primary motive of the attack appeared to be espionage, with the attackers gathering intelligence on government operations and private sector companies.

Long-Term Consequences: The SolarWinds attack highlighted the vulnerabilities of software supply chains and the potential for widespread impact from a single compromised vendor.

Lessons Learned:

Supply Chain Security: The attack emphasized the need for organizations to carefully assess the security of their software supply chains and implement measures to mitigate risks.

Advanced Persistent Threats: The sophisticated techniques used by the attackers demonstrated the increasing capabilities of nation-state actors and the challenges of defending against advanced persistent threats (APTs).

Collaboration and Information Sharing: The incident underscored the importance of collaboration and information sharing between government agencies, private sector companies, and cybersecurity professionals to effectively respond to major cyberattacks.

Tracing attackers: *Cybersecurity professionals can use their expertise to trace cyberattacks back to the perpetrators.*

For example, in the event of a data breach at a financial institution, cybersecurity professionals would work with investigators to identify the source of the breach, assess the damage, and gather evidence to identify the attackers.

Real-World Example: The Bangladesh Bank Heist

One of the most infamous examples of tracing attackers in a cybercrime is the Bangladesh Bank Heist of 2016. This case perfectly illustrates the role of cybersecurity professionals in unraveling a complex attack and identifying the perpetrators.

What Happened:

February 2016: Hackers infiltrated the Bangladesh Bank's systems and used the SWIFT network to send fraudulent transfer requests totaling nearly $1 billion.

The Attack: The attackers exploited vulnerabilities in the bank's security systems and used malware to cover their tracks. They also attempted to delete logs and manipulate databases to hide evidence of their activity.

Losses and Recovery: While most of the fraudulent transactions were blocked, the hackers managed to steal approximately $81 million, transferred to accounts in the Philippines and Sri Lanka.

Tracing the Attackers:

Cybersecurity professionals played a crucial role in investigating the heist. They analyzed malware samples, network logs, and other digital evidence to identify the attackers' methods and tools.

Collaboration with Law Enforcement: Investigators worked with international law enforcement agencies to track the stolen funds and identify the individuals and groups involved.

Attribution: Evidence linked the attack to the Lazarus Group, a cybercrime organization believed to be connected to North Korea. This group has been implicated in several other high-profile cyberattacks.

Lessons Learned:

The Bangladesh Bank heist highlighted the importance of robust cybersecurity measures for financial institutions and the critical role of skilled professionals in investigating and responding to cyberattacks. It also demonstrated the challenges of attribution in cybercrime, as attackers often go to great lengths to obfuscate their identities and origins.

What are some of the emerging trends in cybersecurity that are relevant to financial investigations?

The cybersecurity landscape is constantly evolving, and new threats and vulnerabilities emerge all the time. Some emerging trends in cybersecurity that are relevant to financial investigations include:

Ransomware attacks: Ransomware attacks are becoming increasingly common and sophisticated. Investigators need to be familiar with the latest ransomware variants and techniques to effectively respond to these attacks.

Cloud security: As more financial institutions move their data and operations to the cloud, cloud security is becoming increasingly important. Investigators need to be aware of the unique security challenges associated with cloud computing.

Artificial intelligence (AI) in cybersecurity: AI is being used to develop more sophisticated cybersecurity tools and techniques. Investigators need to be aware of the potential benefits and challenges of using AI in cybersecurity.

By staying informed about the latest cybersecurity trends and collaborating with cybersecurity professionals, financial investigators can effectively combat financial crime in the digital age.

8.4 The Need for Continuous Learning and Adaptation

The field of financial investigations is constantly evolving, driven by the rapid pace of technological advancements and the changing tactics of financial criminals. To remain effective, investigators need to be committed to continuous learning and adaptation.

This involves:

Staying informed about emerging technologies: Investigators need to stay up-to-date on the latest technologies and trends that are relevant to financial crime, such as blockchain technology, artificial intelligence, and cybersecurity.

Developing new skills: Investigators need to continuously develop their skills in digital forensics, data analysis, and other investigative techniques.

Collaboration and knowledge sharing: Investigators should collaborate with other professionals in the field and share knowledge and best practices. This can be done through professional organizations, conferences, and online forums.

Training and professional development: Investigators should participate in regular training and professional development opportunities to stay abreast of the latest trends and techniques in financial investigations.

By embracing a culture of continuous learning and adaptation, investigators can ensure that they are equipped with the knowledge, skills, and tools necessary to effectively combat financial crime in the digital age.

For example, investigators might attend conferences and workshops on blockchain forensics to learn about the latest techniques for tracing cryptocurrency transactions. They might also participate in online forums and communities to share knowledge and best practices with other investigators.

What are some of the challenges associated with continuous learning and adaptation in the field of financial investigations?

The rapid pace of technological change and the evolving tactics of financial criminals can make it challenging for investigators to keep up. Additionally, financial investigations often require specialized knowledge and skills, which can be time-consuming and expensive to acquire.

By prioritizing continuous learning and adaptation, collaborating with other professionals, and seeking out training and professional development opportunities, investigators can overcome these challenges and remain effective in the face of evolving financial crime threats.

8.5 Shaping the Future of Financial Investigations

The future of financial investigations is likely to be shaped by several key trends:

Increased use of technology: Emerging technologies, such as artificial intelligence, machine learning, and blockchain forensics, will continue to play an increasingly important role in financial investigations. These technologies can help investigators analyze vast amounts of data, identify complex patterns, and trace financial transactions more effectively.

Collaboration and information sharing: Collaboration between investigators, financial institutions, and other stakeholders will be crucial for combating financial crime effectively. This includes sharing information about emerging threats, best practices, and investigative techniques.

Cross-border cooperation: As financial crime becomes increasingly globalized, cross-border cooperation between law enforcement agencies and regulatory authorities will be essential for tracing financial transactions and apprehending perpetrators.

Focus on prevention: In addition to investigating financial crimes after they occur, there will be a growing emphasis on preventing financial crime through education, awareness campaigns, and proactive measures.

Investigators who embrace these trends and adapt their strategies and techniques accordingly will be well-positioned to combat financial crime effectively in the future.

For example, investigators might use AI-powered tools to analyze large datasets of financial transactions and identify suspicious activity in real-time. They might also collaborate with financial institutions to share information about emerging threats and develop proactive measures to prevent financial crimes.

What are some of the key challenges and opportunities that will shape the future of financial investigations?

The future of financial investigations presents both challenges and opportunities. The increasing sophistication of financial criminals and the rapid pace of technological change will continue to challenge investigators. However, emerging technologies also offer new opportunities to combat financial crime more effectively. By embracing collaboration, information sharing, and a focus on prevention, investigators can shape the future of financial investigations and stay ahead of the curve in the fight against financial crime.

Conclusion

In this era where the digital and financial realms are increasingly intertwined, the internet has emerged as both a fertile ground for financial criminals and a potent arsenal for those dedicated to upholding financial integrity. Throughout this book, we've embarked on a comprehensive exploration of how the internet can be harnessed in the relentless pursuit of financial crimes, offering a beacon of hope in a landscape often shadowed by complexity and concealment.

The internet's role in the metamorphosis of financial crime cannot be overstated. It has dismantled geographical barriers, accelerated transactions, and cloaked illicit activities in layers of anonymity. Yet, in this evolution lies the very essence of opportunity for investigators. By understanding the nuances of cybercrime, the nature of digital evidence, and the vast expanse of the internet's resources, investigators are equipped with a formidable toolkit to dismantle the mechanisms of financial malfeasance.

Digital evidence stands as the keystone in the architecture of financial investigations. Its integrity, relevance, and clarity are pivotal in the construction of a robust investigative narrative. As we've delved into the intricacies of digital evidence, it's become evident that mastering its collection, preservation, and presentation is not just a skill but an imperative in the digital age. This evidence, when wielded with expertise, can illuminate the darkest corners of financial crimes, offering clarity amidst obfuscation.

Open Source Intelligence (OSINT) has been unveiled as a critical asset in the investigative arsenal. The vast reservoirs of publicly available information, when navigated with discernment, can unravel complex financial schemes and unveil the actors behind them. OSINT is not merely about gathering data; it's about weaving disparate threads of information into a coherent narrative, providing insights that are often hidden in plain sight.

The exploration of cryptocurrency investigations has underscored the dual nature of this digital currency phenomenon. While cryptocurrencies present new avenues for criminals, they also offer innovative pathways for investigations. Understanding the blockchain, deciphering the flow of digital currencies, and leveraging forensic tools are essential skills in the modern investigator's repertoire, enabling them to trace transactions that were once considered untraceable.

Advancements in investigative techniques and technologies are at the vanguard of the fight against financial crime. Artificial intelligence, machine learning, and advanced analytics have emerged as powerful allies in deciphering complex data patterns and predicting criminal trajectories. These technologies, when harnessed with precision, can amplify the impact of investigations, turning vast seas of data into actionable intelligence.

The journey through the legal and ethical landscapes has highlighted the paramount importance of conducting investigations within the bounds of law and morality. In an age where privacy concerns are ever-present, maintaining a balance between investigative rigor and respect for individual rights is a delicate but essential endeavor. The legal frameworks and ethical principles discussed serve as a compass, guiding investigators through the challenging terrain of digital financial investigations.

The theme of collaboration has resonated throughout this book, underscoring the importance of synergy among investigators, legal experts, technologists, and international partners. In a domain where knowledge is power, collective efforts amplify the capacity to confront and conquer financial crimes.

As we gaze into the future, it's clear that the landscape of financial investigations will continue to evolve, shaped by the relentless march of technology and the ingenuity of financial criminals. The horizon is filled with both challenges and opportunities. To navigate this ever-changing terrain, investigators must embrace a mindset of continuous learning, adaptability, and proactive engagement with emerging technologies.

The journey does not end here; it merely transforms. The future beckons with the promise of more sophisticated tools, deeper insights, and broader collaborations. As investigators, the commitment to excellence, integrity, and relentless pursuit of justice remains the guiding star.

In closing, this book is not just a repository of knowledge; it's a call to action. It's an invitation to financial investigators to rise to the challenges of the digital age, to wield the power of the internet with wisdom and courage, and to ensure that in the vast and intricate tapestry of the financial world, integrity remains the golden thread.

In the quest to uphold financial integrity, let this book be both your guide and your inspiration, empowering you to harness the digital frontier in the relentless pursuit of justice and security in the financial landscape of tomorrow.

References

Cybersecurity Ventures. (2023). Cybercrime Report 2023. https://cybersecurityventures.com/cybercrime-report-2023/

European Union. (2018). General Data Protection Regulation (GDPR). https://gdpr.eu/

California Department of Justice. (2018). California Consumer Privacy Act (CCPA). https://oag.ca.gov/privacy/ccpa

Financial Action Task Force (FATF). (2023). International Standards on Combating Money Laundering and the Financing of Terrorism & Proliferation. https://www.fatf-gafi.org/publications/fatfrecommendations/documents/fatf-recommendations.html

Reiter, K. D. (2018). Blockchain and the Law: Theory and Practice. Routledge.

Casey, E. (2019). Digital Evidence and Computer Crime: Forensic Science, Computers and the Internet. Routledge.

The Association of Certified Fraud Examiners (ACFE). (2022). Report to the Nations: 2022 Global Study on Occupational Fraud and Abuse. https://www.acfe.com/report-to-the-nations/2022

United States Department of Justice. (2023). Cybercrime. https://www.justice.gov/criminal-ccips/cybercrime

Federal Bureau of Investigation (FBI). (2023). Cyber Crime. https://www.fbi.gov/investigate/cyber

Securities and Exchange Commission (SEC). (2023). Cybersecurity and Investor Protection. https://www.sec.gov/divisions/enforce/cybersecurity.htm

Internal Revenue Service (IRS). (2023). Tax Fraud & Other Financial Crimes. https://www.irs.gov/compliance/criminal-investigation

The World Bank. (2023). Financial Crime and Corruption. https://www.worldbank.org/en/topic/governance/brief/anti-money-laundering-and-combating-the-financing-of-terrorism

The United Nations Office on Drugs and Crime (UNODC). (2023). Cybercrime. https://www.unodc.org/unodc/en/cybercrime/what-is-cybercrime.html

The International Criminal Police Organization (INTERPOL). (2023). Cybercrime. https://www.interpol.int/en/Crimes/Cybercrime

The European Union Agency for Cybersecurity (ENISA). (2023). Cybersecurity Threats and Trends. https://www.enisa.europa.eu/publications/threat-landscape-2023

The National Institute of Standards and Technology (NIST). (2023). Cybersecurity Framework. https://www.nist.gov/cyberframework

The SANS Institute. (2023). SANS 2023 Top New Attacks and Threats. https://www.sans.org/critical-security-controls

The Cloud Security Alliance (CSA). (2023). The Treacherous 12 Cloud Computing Top Threats in 2023. https://cloudsecurityalliance.org/research/top-threats/

The Open Web Application Security Project (OWASP). (2023). OWASP Top 10 Web Application Security Risks. https://owasp.org/www-project-top-ten/

The Center for Strategic and International Studies (CSIS). (2023). Cybersecurity and Financial Stability. https://www.csis.org/programs/international-security-program/projects/cybersecurity-and-financial-stability

The Financial Stability Board (FSB). (2023). Cyber Risk and Resilience in the Financial System. https://www.fsb.org/work-of-the-fsb/policy-development/cyber-risk-and-resilience-in-the-financial-system/

www.ingramcontent.com/pod-product-compliance
Lightning Source LLC
Chambersburg PA
CBHW052201220526
45471CB00004B/1758